BRITISH AIRCRAFT
OF WORLD WAR I

BRITISH AIRCRAFT OF WORLD WAR I
1914–18

EDWARD WARD

amber
BOOKS

First published in 2024

Copyright © 2024 Amber Books Ltd

All rights reserved. No part of this publication may be reproduced, stored in a retrieval system, or transmitted in any form or by any means, electronic, mechanical, photocopying, recording, or otherwise, without prior written permission of the copyright holder.

Amber Books Ltd
United House
North Road
London N7 9DP
United Kingdom
www.amberbooks.co.uk
Facebook: amberbooks
YouTube: amberbooksltd
Instagram: amberbooksltd
X(Twitter): @amberbooks

ISBN: 978-1-83886-478-1

Editor: Michael Spilling
Design: Andrew Easton & Mark Batley
Picture research: Terry Forshaw
Illustrator: Ronny Bar

Printed in China

Contents

Introduction	6
Single-Seat Fighters	8
Two-Seater Fighters & Reconnaissance	48
Bombers	84
Flying Boats, Seaplanes & Airships	108
INDEX	124
PICTURE CREDITS	128

Introduction

As was the case in other nations, British aircraft were primitive and ineffectual at the outbreak of the conflict, but would undergo a remarkable transformation over the following four years, ending the war with a huge aircraft industry supplying the RAF with some of the finest aircraft designs in the world.

The United Kingdom entered World War I with two separate air arms, the Army's Royal Flying Corps and the Royal Naval Air Service. Early types concentrated on two-seat, general-purpose aircraft that could be utilized for any duty, within reason, that was required of them, though the primary duties of the RFC at the outbreak of the war were artillery cooperation and photographic reconnaissance. The crucial nature of this work became swiftly apparent when, on 22 August 1914, aerial reconnaissance revealed von Kluck's 1st German Army poised to outflank the British Expeditionary Force, cutting it from its supply lines. This was contradictory to existing intelligence but was swiftly acted upon by General John French, who ordered the retreat to Mons, saving tens of thousands of British soldiers from captivity or death.

British aircraft soon came into contact with enemy machines, and aerial fighting became more commonplace, the intensity of which inevitably increased over the next few years. In 1915, the RFC introduced the first dedicated fighter, the two-seat Vickers Gunbus, and the first British single-seat fighter, the D.H.2 appeared at the front in early 1916. Later developments would see the RFC develop a sophisticated system of army cooperation and ground attack. The latter proved highly effective but involved extremely high losses, approaching 30 per cent of aircraft so committed.

Royal Naval Air Service
Meanwhile, the RNAS initially saw its primary roles as fleet reconnaissance, maritime patrols searching for enemy ships, submarines, and zeppelins, and attacking enemy coastal installations. As the war progressed, however, the RNAS saw its roles progressively widen. It maintained fighter squadrons

Sopwith Camels ranged on the flight deck of HMS *Furious*. By the end of the war Britain had carried out the first carrier strike in history and possessed a huge lead over other nations in the realm of naval aviation.

INTRODUCTION

The Felixstowe F.2 was the most powerful and effective flying boat to see action during the conflict. Initially, maritime patrol was seen as the preserve of the airship but aircraft such as the Felixstowe flying boats began the inexorable shift of this role to conventional aircraft.

in France to support the RFC, devised airborne escorts for convoys using airships, developed aircraft carriers, both of seaplanes and landplanes, and the aircraft to equip them, as well as initiating and developing a land-based strategic bomber force, something the RFC, primarily concerned with the tactical support of the army in the field, had no great interest in pursuing.

The existence of two large aviation forces led to inevitable interservice rivalry and even problematic procurement issues. For example, the Sopwith company were under an exclusive contract with the Admiralty, so RNAS squadrons enjoyed priority for the latest fighter designs, such as Sopwith Pups and Camels as they appeared and regardless of need.

Merger

The logistical problems of the two services were, however, effectively solved on 1 April 1918 by merging the RFC and RNAS into one organization to create the Royal Air Force, the world's first independent air arm. The final year of the war would see British air power at its most potent, both on land, with RAF aircraft proving instrumental at the decisive Battle of Amiens, and at sea, as the first carrier strike in history was flown by Camels from HMS *Furious*.

Technical lead

The British aircraft industry was in the vanguard of technical development, and new aircraft were appearing that promised even greater combat performance, such as the Martinsyde F.4 Buzzard fighter, which possessed a terrific turn of speed; the armoured ground-attack Sopwith Salamander, which pre-empted such aircraft as the Il-2 Sturmovik of World War II; and the Handley Page V/1500, a four-engined bomber that could attack Berlin from bases in eastern England. All were in production by November 1918 and entering squadron service, but none would be used operationally during the conflict.

SINGLE-SEAT FIGHTERS

SINGLE-SEAT FIGHTERS

Although British squadrons relied heavily on French aircraft, particularly Nieuport Scouts, for their fighter needs, the homegrown D.H.2 was the world's first aircraft specifically designed from the outset to be a single-seat fighter. Later in the war, newer British designs would come to the fore, including the classic pairing of Sopwith Camel and S.E.5a. The following aircraft are featured in this chapter:

- Sopwith Tabloid and Schneider
- Bristol Scout
- Martinsyde Scout
- Airco DH.2
- Morane-Saulnier Type N
- Early Nieuport Scouts
- Nieuport 17, 21 and 23
- Nieuport 24 and 27
- Vickers FB.19
- Sopwith Pup
- Airco DH.5
- Royal Aircraft Factory F.E.8
- Bristol M.1
- Sopwith Triplane
- SPAD S.VII
- Sopwith Camel
- Royal Aircraft Factory S.E.5 and S.E.5a
- SPAD S.XIII
- Sopwith 5F.1 Dolphin
- Sopwith Snipe

Flight Lt. Frederick Rutland takes off in a Sopwith Pup from the flying-off platform mounted on one of the gun turrets of the cruiser HMS *Yarmouth* on 28 June 1917, the first such launch of an aircraft in history.

SINGLE-SEAT FIGHTERS

Sopwith Tabloid and Schneider

One of the most successful of the early single-seaters, the Tabloid was comparatively fast and nimble and served both on land and, as the Sopwith Schneider, as a naval floatplane.

First flown in 1913 as a two-seat sports aircraft, with pilot and passenger unusually seated side by side, the Tabloid (so named due to its diminutive size) demonstrated impressive speed and climb. Its performance was such that it was reworked as a single-seat floatplane and entered the prestigious Schneider Trophy contest of 1914, which it duly won. The RNAS ordered 12 floatplanes, named the Sopwith Schneider in honour of its race-winning credentials, in November 1914, and eventually would take delivery of 136 examples.

Wartime action

The Tabloid also secured a military order, with 36 single-seat landplanes being built for both the RFC and RNAS. These were used, like the contemporary Bristol Scout, as fast, general-purpose machines and were amongst the earliest British single-seaters to be armed when individual aircraft began to be fitted with improvised machine gun mountings. Several RNAS Tabloids were fitted with a Lewis gun on the top wing, firing above the propeller arc, and at least one was equipped with deflector wedges on the propeller blades to allow a fuselage-mounted machine gun to fire directly forwards. More dramatically, however, the Tabloid made history by becoming the first British aircraft to mount a bombing raid on Germany on 22 September, following this up with a successful attack on Zeppelin facilities. On 8 October, four Tabloids flew from Antwerp to bomb Zeppelin sheds at Cologne and Dusseldorf. The two aircraft sent to Cologne were unable to locate the target, but the Dusseldorf Zeppelin hangar was struck by two 9.1kg (20lb) bombs dropped from 180m (600ft), destroying Zeppelin LZ 25 within.

Sopwith Tabloid

Weight (Maximum take-off): 580kg (1120lb)
Dimensions: Length 6.2m (20ft 4in), Wingspan 7.77m (25ft 6in), Height 3.05m (10ft)
Powerplant: one 75kW (100hp) Gnome Monosoupape nine-cylinder air-cooled rotary piston engine
Maximum speed: 148km/h (92mph)
Endurance: 3 hours 30 minutes
Ceiling: 4572m (15,000ft)
Crew: one
Armament: one 7.7mm (0.303in) Lewis machine gun fitted to some RNAS machines; bombload of up to two 9.1kg (20lb) Cooper bombs

---

Sopwith Tabloid

One of the first two Tabloids to reach the front, No. 168 took part in the raid on German Zeppelin sheds at Dusseldorf of 8 October 1914. Flown by Flight Lieutenant Reggie Marix, the aircraft ran out of fuel 32km (20 miles) short of its home airfield and Marix had to borrow a bicycle in order to return to base.

SINGLE-SEAT FIGHTERS

Bristol Scout

The Bristol Scout never fully realized its potential due to the lack of a means to fire the gun directly forwards. Despite this impediment, it achieved some success and made history by performing the first take-off by a landplane from an aircraft carrier.

Designed by Frank Barnwell and an excellent aircraft for its era, the Scout was derived, like many of the early single-seaters, from a pre-war racing design. First flown in February 1914, the Scout demonstrated an impressive speed of 157km/h (97.5mph) during evaluation by the Army at Farnborough. Although this aircraft was lost during the London-Paris-London race in July, its performance was promising enough to warrant further development, and two further Scouts were under construction when war broke out, which were requisitioned by the War Office. Nicknamed Bristol 'Bullets' due to their high speed, the two Scouts were highly regarded, and one was armed with a rifle on each side of the fuselage, obliquely angled to fire forward and to the side. Orders were placed for more Scouts by both the Army and Navy, all unarmed as delivered, though various armament fits were extemporized at unit level.

Notable users
One such Scout was fitted with an archaic Martini single-shot carbine firing obliquely to starboard and was used by Major Lanoe Hawker to force down three machine-gun-armed German aircraft during a single patrol on the evening of 25 July 1915. For this feat, Hawker was awarded the Victoria Cross. Meanwhile, fear of Zeppelin attack led to the idea of launching Scouts from ships at sea, and on 3 November 1915, the first take-off from the deck of HMS *Vindex* was made by Flight-Lt. Towler in a Bristol Scout. Ultimately, only one Zeppelin was intercepted by a Bristol Scout from HMS *Vindex*. Armed only with Ranken darts, these were released on the airship, but no damage was caused.

Bristol Scout
Weight (Maximum take-off): 542kg (1195lb)
Dimensions: Length 6.3m (20ft 8in), Wingspan 7.49m (24ft 7in), Height 2.59m (8ft 6in)
Powerplant: one 60kW (80hp) Le Rhône 9C nine-cylinder air-cooled rotary piston engine
Maximum speed: 151km/h (94mph)
Endurance: 2 hours 30 minutes
Ceiling: 4900m (16,000ft)
Crew: one
Armament: one 7.7mm (0.303in) Lewis gun sometimes fitted above top wing, various extemporized rifles and other small arms; up to 48 0.45kg (1lb) Ranken explosive flechettes

---

Bristol Scout
One of five Bristol Scouts sent to the Eastern Mediterranean in 1915, No.1264 served with No. 2 Wing RNAS on the island of Imbros. The initial RNAS roundel was a red ring with a white centre. In 1915, this was modified, as here, with a blue dot to more readily conform with other Allied aircraft.

SINGLE-SEAT FIGHTERS

Martinsyde Scout

Inspired by the Sopwith Tabloid and Bristol Scout, the Martinsyde S.1 was a relatively mediocre machine which nonetheless performed important pioneering work in the first year of the war.

The Martin & Handasyde company had produced a series of modestly successful monoplanes in the years immediately prior to the outbreak of hostilities under the Martinsyde name, but after the Sopwith Tabloid and Bristol Scout demonstrated that a well-designed biplane was able to outperform contemporary monoplanes, Martinsyde responded with the S.1, its first tractor biplane.

Unbeloved of pilots
Utterly conventional for its time, apart from the unusual and somewhat clumsy four-wheel undercarriage fitted to the first production machines, the Martinsyde Scout possessed an inferior performance to the Tabloid, which utilized the same engine due to its greater size. However, the Martinsyde, as supplied by the factory, was able to be fitted with a fixed Lewis gun on the top wing, firing directly forward over the top of the propeller. It is not known when the S.1 made its first flight, but the aircraft was ordered into production, and 11 had been built by the end of 1914. Like its more successful counterpart, the Bristol Scout, the Martinsyde never equipped an entire squadron, but was issued piecemeal to RFC units on the Western Front.

Its pedestrian performance and lack of stability did not endear it to pilots, the Bristol aircraft being much preferred, but the Martinsyde did see some combat action, including one particularly hair-raising incident on 10 May 1915. Attacking a German two-seater, Captain Louis Strange found the Lewis gun's ammunition drum had jammed. Strange stood up to change the drum with the control column between his knees, but the machine turned upside down. Strange fell out but managed to hang on to the Lewis gun and was left dangling underneath his inverted aircraft. Fortunately, the drum did not come off, and amazingly, he was able to hook his feet back in the cockpit and right the aircraft after spinning down for more than 1500m (5000ft).

During the summer of 1915 the Martinsyde Scout was withdrawn from France, but a handful continued operations in Mesopotamia, with one supplying reconnaissance of Turkish positions leading directly to the capture of the city of Kut in September 1915.

Martinsyde Scout
Weight (Maximum take-off): 550kg (1213lb)
Dimensions: Length 6.4m (21ft), Wingspan 8.43m (27ft 8in), Height 2.5m (8ft 2in)
Powerplant: one 60kW (80hp) Gnome Lambda seven-cylinder air-cooled rotary piston engine
Maximum speed: 140km/h (87mph)
Endurance: 2 hours 30 minutes
Ceiling: 4800m (15,750ft)
Crew: one
Armament: optional 7.7mm (0.303in) Lewis machine gun fixed firing forward on upper wing centre section

An immaculate factory-fresh Martinsyde Scout, Serial No. 4241, displays the later, and much tidier, two-wheeled undercarriage that replaced the four wheeled unit fitted to earlier production machines.

SINGLE-SEAT FIGHTERS

Airco DH.2

The world's first purpose-designed single-seat fighter, the DH.2 overcame an unfortunate early reputation to emerge as an excellent fighting scout and the machine of choice for most early British aces.

Airco DH.2

This DH.2 was on the strength of No. 24 Sqn RFC, the first British squadron to be equipped with the type. 24 Sqn was based at Bertangles aerodrome, a short distance north of Amiens.

Often described as a response to the appearance of the Fokker Eindecker, development of the DH.2 had in fact started before the Eindecker appeared over the front. Lacking any kind of synchronizer to allow a machine gun to fire through the propeller disc, a pusher layout was adopted by designer Geoffrey de Havilland for the DH.2 to allow a machine gun to fire directly forwards. Essentially a scaled-down development of the earlier two-seat DH.1, the DH.2 flew for the first time on 1 July 1915 and, as was then customary, the prototype was despatched to the front for trials under service conditions, arriving in France at the end of the same month. Despite the loss of this aircraft, which was shot down and captured sufficiently intact that it was repaired and evaluated by German forces, the DH.2 was ordered into production with the first machines accepted by the Flying Corps in December 1915. The first RFC unit to be wholly equipped with single seaters, 24 squadron, flew its DH.2s to France in February 1916.

Mixed reputation

Although possessing an excellent rate of climb for its day and outclassing the Eindecker in both speed and manoeuvrability, the DH.2 was initially regarded with some trepidation by its pilots. The controls of the aircraft were very sensitive, and the aircraft gained a reputation for falling into an unheralded spin, a condition from which recovery was then believed to be impossible, and the DH.2 earned the grim nickname of 'The Spinning Incinerator'.

Experience proved, however, that the evil reputation of the type was unfounded. Much of the credit for this change can be attributed to Lt Sidney Cowan of 24 squadron, who was the first to demonstrate aerobatics in the DH.2 and was eventually to score seven victories on the type. The DH.2 was not flawless, however – the Gnome engine was known to occasionally shed cylinders, which could then smash into the tail booms with catastrophic results. At least two pilots lost their lives due to such failures, and another two were lucky to survive.

Airco DH.2

Weight (Maximum take-off): 654kg (1441lb)
Dimensions: Length 7.68m (25ft 3in), Wingspan 8.61m (28ft 3in), Height 2.92m (9ft 7in)
Powerplant: one 75kW (100hp) Gnome Monosoupape 9-cylinder air-cooled rotary piston engine
Maximum speed: 150km/h (93mph)
Endurance: 2 hours 45 minutes
Ceiling: 4300m (14,000ft)
Crew: one
Armament: one 7.7mm (0.303in) Lewis machine gun fixed forward firing in nose

Successful in operations

In combat, the DH.2 proved highly successful, and most of the first RFC aces would score some or all of their victories with the type. Furthermore, the DH.2 units quickly gained a reputation for almost wilfully aggressive flying. To give just one example, on 15 September 1916, three DH.2s attacked 17 enemy aircraft, shot down two and drove off the remainder. Operational experience saw the flexible gun mounting, the pilot initially being expected to aim the gun whilst

SINGLE-SEAT FIGHTERS

simultaneously flying the aircraft, giving way to a rigidly fixed weapon as would be standard on virtually every subsequent single-seat fighter. By the end of 1916, however, new German fighters of greater performance outclassed the DH.2, which began to be replaced by Nieuport scouts from March 1916, although DH.2s remained operational with Home Defence squadrons and in Palestine until the autumn of 1917. Four hundred and twenty-three DH.2s were built, and the most successful DH.2 pilot was Patrick Langan-Byrne, an Irish ace who scored all 10 of his victories with the type.

Photographed at Beauval in 1916, pilots of No.32 Sqn RFC pose in front of one of the squadron's DH.2s; 32 Sqn would fly the Airco pusher until re-equipping in May 1917 with the DH.5.

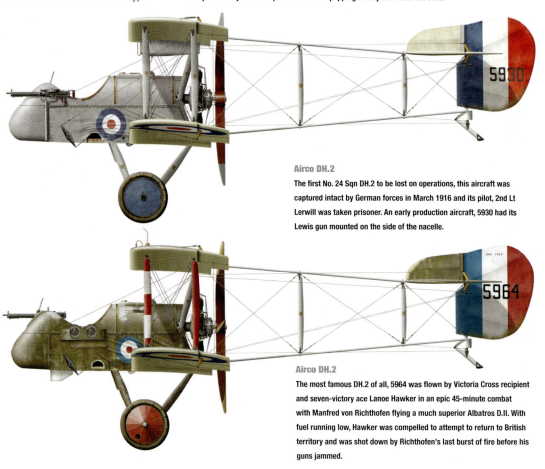

Airco DH.2

The first No. 24 Sqn DH.2 to be lost on operations, this aircraft was captured intact by German forces in March 1916 and its pilot, 2nd Lt Lerwill was taken prisoner. An early production aircraft, 5930 had its Lewis gun mounted on the side of the nacelle.

Airco DH.2

The most famous DH.2 of all, 5964 was flown by Victoria Cross recipient and seven-victory ace Lanoe Hawker in an epic 45-minute combat with Manfred von Richthofen flying a much superior Albatros D.II. With fuel running low, Hawker was compelled to attempt to return to British territory and was shot down by Richthofen's last burst of fire before his guns jammed.

SINGLE-SEAT FIGHTERS

Morane-Saulnier Type N

Although only a small number of the Type N and its derivatives were produced, the aircraft was significant as the first true single-seat fighter to be operated by the Allies.

The Type N was conceived and built in 1914 as a racing aircraft, but after war broke out, it was developed for military use. Despite its speed, it was never particularly popular with service pilots due to its demanding handling characteristics. Control was by wing-warping in the lateral plane, and the horizontal tail surfaces were all-moving. The latter feature rendered the Type N undeniably responsive but required constant attention just to keep the aircraft flying straight and level. However, the most important innovation of the aircraft was its armament, fitted from the start with a machine gun directly behind the propeller. The aircraft was equipped with triangular steel deflector plates on the propeller blades so that any bullet that would otherwise hit the propeller was deflected off. This system was crude and prone to failure but, for the first time, allowed a pilot of a conventional tractor aircraft to aim the entire fighter at its target. The prototype entered service with the French in June 1915, with production machines appearing in

Morane-Solnier Type N
This Type N formed part of the equipment of No. 1 Sqn RFC in late 1915 and early 1916. It was lost in combat with a German two-seater on 9 March 1916.

the same month, but the introduction of the Nieuport 11, which did not require the unreliable deflector plate system and was far easier to fly, saw the Type N discarded by French units by the end of the year.

Bright red noses
The RFC made considerably greater use of their Type Ns, though the type only ever partially equipped two squadrons. Following the appearance of the Fokker Eindecker, the RFC found itself chronically short of single-seat scouts (in June 1915, only nine such aircraft were at the front), and the first Type Ns, named 'Bullet' in British service, were received in September. Although the flying qualities of the N were viewed with some anxiety, the type proved modestly successful on operations, and in a mock combat

Morane-Saulnier Type N
Weight (Maximum take-off): 444kg (979lb)
Dimensions: Length 5.83m (19ft 2in), Wingspan 8.15m (26ft 9in), Height 2.25m (7ft 5in)
Powerplant: one 60kW (80hp) Le Rhône 9C nine-cylinder air-cooled rotary piston engine
Maximum speed: 144km/h (89 mph)
Endurance: 1 hour 30 minutes
Ceiling: 4000m (13,000ft)
Crew: one
Armament: one 7.7mm (0.303in) Vickers machine gun fixed firing forward on fuselage decking

held between a Bullet and a captured Eindecker, the Morane totally outclassed the German machine. Later aircraft were delivered with more powerful Le Rhone engines, and following the opening of the Somme campaign, all RFC Bullets featured bright red noses to allow them to be easily identified by AA gunners who were accustomed to assume any monoplane scout must be German. With the appearance of better fighters at the front, the last Type Ns of the RFC were withdrawn to home defence and training units in October 1916.

SINGLE-SEAT FIGHTERS

Early Nieuport scouts

A remarkably successful fighter, the Nieuport Scout, as the various iterations of the Nieuport design were collectively known, effectively ended the 'Fokker Scourge' and served in every Allied fighter arm.

As with many other early war fighters, the basic Nieuport design derived from a pre-war racing aircraft, intended for the 1914 Gordon Bennett Cup. Following the outbreak of war, the design was reworked into a two-seat reconnaissance aircraft as the Nieuport 10, entering service in 1915. The racing origins of the Nieuport led its designer Gustave Delage to investigate a distinctive layout on the quest for higher speed wherein the lower wing possessed a much smaller area than the upper wing. This was intended to combine the strength, compactness and stability of the biplane with the speed of the monoplane. Known as a 'sesquiplane', the design featured a highly distinctive vee-shaped wing strut and was to prove hugely influential.

Configuration of variants

Some Nieuport 10s were built as single-seaters, with the front cockpit faired over, to become the first of Nieuport's classic fighters, with a single Vickers or Lewis gun arranged to fire upwards above the propeller or with a Lewis gun mounted to the top wing firing directly forwards. The Nieuport 10 proved successful enough as a single-seat fighter for a purpose-designed single-seat variant to be developed, the Nieuport 11. Of smaller size than its forebear, the Nieuport 11 was one of the smallest combat aircraft ever built leading to its diminutive nickname of 'Bebe'. Entering service in January 1916, the Nieuport 11 was superior to the Fokker Eindecker in every regard. Re-engined with a more powerful Le Rhone 9J engine, the aircraft design became the Nieuport 16, which was built in even greater numbers.

Both the Nieuport 10 and 11 were utilized by the RNAS, and the later Nieuport 16 was operated by the RFC. The last British-operated examples of these early Nieuport Scouts were withdrawn from the Western Front in April 1917. A further two-seat development of the Nieuport 10 was also developed as the Nieuport 12 with a more powerful engine and larger top wing and utilized for reconnaissance, fighting and artillery spotting before enjoying a long career as a successful training aircraft. The Nieuport 12 was the first of the Nieuport line to be built under licence in Britain, with 50 completed by Beardmore.

Nieuport 16
Weight (Maximum take-off): 550kg (1213lb)
Dimensions: Length 6.4m (21ft), Wingspan 8.43m (27ft 8in), Height 2.5m (8ft 2in)
Powerplant: one 60kW (80hp) Gnome Lambda seven-cylinder air-cooled rotary piston engine
Maximum speed: 140km/h (87mph)
Endurance: 2 hours 30 minutes
Ceiling: 4800m (15,750ft)
Crew: one
Armament: optional 7.7mm (0.303in) Lewis machine gun fixed firing forward on upper wing centre section

---

Nieuport 16
Nieuport 16 A125 was delivered to No. 60 Sqn RFC in August 1916 but was shot down on 3 November by Hans Immelmann of Jasta 2.

SINGLE-SEAT FIGHTERS

Nieuport 17, 21 and 23

Developed from the Nieuport 11, the 17 was probably the best fighter in the world on its debut. Built in enormous numbers, the Nieuport 17 proved even more successful than its predecessors and served in every Allied air arm.

Seeking to improve on his popular Nieuport 11 design, Gustave Delage concurrently developed the Nieuport 16, which was little more than a re-engined 11, and the more thoroughly redesigned Nieuport 17. The latter featured the same Le Rhône 9J engine as the Nieuport 16 but complemented it with a redesigned, slightly larger airframe of improved aerodynamic form and longer wings for better handling. Apart from the very first examples, the Nie 17 also featured the Alkan-Hamy synchronization gear and could thus discard the somewhat clumsy top wing-mounted Lewis gun armament.

Combat debut

First flying in January 1916, the new Nieuport was in service by March, though it was only in May that the first French squadron was entirely equipped with the type. By late 1916, however, every French fighter squadron was equipped with the Nieuport 17, and the type was utilized by virtually every French ace of note to score at least some of their victories.

International interest

The aircraft's obvious merit saw it eagerly acquired by other nations, with several also producing it under licence, notably Italy and Russia, who both produced substantial totals of the aircraft. Even the Germans paid the aircraft the ultimate compliment by producing and operating an unlicensed copy as the Siemens-Schuckert D.I. In the UK, the Nieuport 17's marked superiority over any equivalent British type did not go unnoticed, and the aircraft was acquired in large numbers for both the RFC and RNAS. In addition, the Nieuport & General Aircraft Company Ltd was formed near London specifically to produce it under licence. British Nieuports initially featured either the synchronized Vickers gun or a Lewis gun on a Foster mount on the

Nieuport 17
Weight (Maximum take-off): 560kg (1235lb)
Dimensions: Length 5.8m (19ft 0in), Wingspan 8.16m (26ft 9in), Height 2.4m (7ft 10in)
Powerplant: one 82kW (110hp) Le Rhône 9Ja nine-cylinder air-cooled rotary piston engine
Maximum speed: 170km/h (110mph)
Endurance: 1 hour 45 minutes
Ceiling: 5300m (17,400ft)
Crew: one
Armament: one 7.7mm (0.303in) Lewis machine gun fixed, firing forward on top wing, provision for eight air-to-air Le Prieur rockets fitted to interplane struts

top wing before standardizing on the latter, due to its light weight, higher rate of fire and simplicity in November 1916. British Nieuports also featured a strengthened lower wing spar construction following several incidents wherein the aircraft lost one or both lower wings. This failure was caused by the lower wing twisting under aerodynamic load, leading to a failure

Nieuport 17
One of the most successful exponents of the Nieuport Scout, Captain Albert Ball scored 11 of his eventual total of 44 victories with this Nieuport 17, to which he had fitted the prominent red propeller spinner.

17

SINGLE-SEAT FIGHTERS

of the collar holding the lower wing to the interplane vee strut. Provided the rigging held and the top wing remained in place, the aircraft remained controllable, and several pilots experienced such a failure and lived to tell the tale, amongst them the top-scoring British ace Edward Mannock, but others were not so lucky. Separate modifications were undertaken to prevent this problem independently in both France and the UK. This problem had little effect on the general career of the Nieuport 17, however, which was proving both highly effective and popular with pilots.

Many British and Commonwealth aces were to fly the Nieuport in action, most famously perhaps the Canadian William Avery Bishop, who won the Victoria Cross for a controversial solo mission behind enemy lines in which he claimed three German aircraft destroyed. Top scorer of Nieuport Scout pilots of any nation, however, was Phillip Fullard, who achieved 40 victories in Nieuports, half of them in the Nieuport 17.

Variants and derivatives

The Nieuport 17's success, large production run (though no records survive of how many were produced, the total is estimated at around 3000) and simplicity saw it used as the basis for further variants, which were little changed to the base model. The Nieuport 17bis was a British derivative produced by the Nieuport and General company featuring a fuselage of improved aerodynamic shape, which would later be used on the Nieuport 24 and 27 and fitted with the 97kW (130hp) Clerget 9B due to shortages of Le Rhone engines.

The larger circumference of the Clerget resulted in a distinctive 'ballooned' cowling, allowing easy identification of the type. The aircraft was used primarily by the RNAS and found to have a performance broadly akin to Sopwith's Triplane.

Nieuport 23

Meanwhile, in France, Nieuport produced the lightened Nieuport 21 equipped with a lower-powered 60kW (80hp) Le Rhône rotary engine, to allow for a greater range in the escort role. Externally identifiable by its horseshoe cowling and lacking a pilot's headrest, the Nie 21 was seldom used in its intended role but was widely employed as a general fighter alongside the standard Nie 17, though only a very few entered British service. The slightly later Nieuport 23 differed only in some points of its internal structure and in its use of a different gun synchronizer, and in all other respects was identical to the Nie 17. To somewhat confuse matters, however, the Nie 23bis, similar to the earlier Nie 17bis, utilized the fuselage of the Nie 24 but married to standard Nie 17 flying surfaces and a Le Rhone engine. The most radical development of the basic aircraft, however, was the Nieuport triplane, of which two were built derived from a Nie 17 and 17bis respectively. Possessing an extremely unusual arrangement with the uppermost of the three wings fitted with an extreme back stagger, the triplanes were found to have an excellent rate of climb but problematic handling meant production was not undertaken.

Nieuport 23
Weight (Maximum take-off): 574kg (1263lb)
Dimensions: Length 6.4m (21ft), Wingspan 8.2m (26ft 11in), Height 2.4m (7ft 11in)
Powerplant: one 90kW (120hp) Le Rhône 9Jb nine-cylinder air-cooled rotary piston engine
Maximum speed: 168km/h (105mph)
Endurance: 1 hour 7 minutes
Ceiling: 6500m (21,000ft)
Crew: one
Armament: one 7.7mm (0.303in) Lewis machine gun mounted above top wing centre section

SINGLE-SEAT FIGHTERS

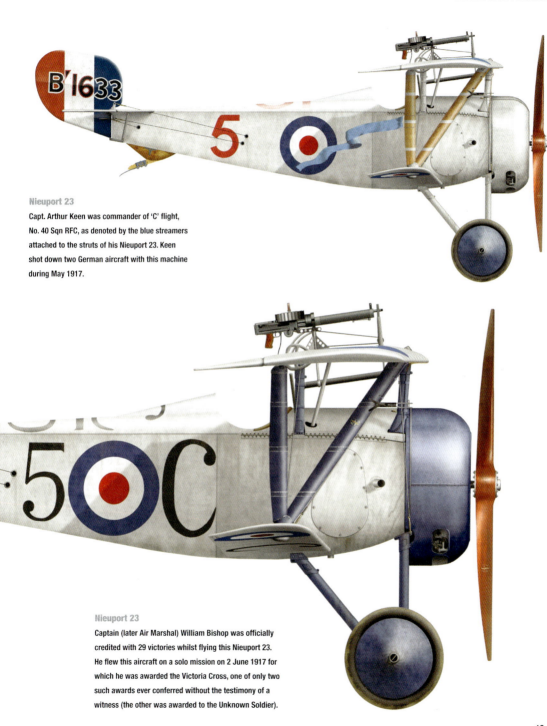

Nieuport 23
Capt. Arthur Keen was commander of 'C' flight, No. 40 Sqn RFC, as denoted by the blue streamers attached to the struts of his Nieuport 23. Keen shot down two German aircraft with this machine during May 1917.

Nieuport 23
Captain (later Air Marshal) William Bishop was officially credited with 29 victories whilst flying this Nieuport 23. He flew this aircraft on a solo mission on 2 June 1917 for which he was awarded the Victoria Cross, one of only two such awards ever conferred without the testimony of a witness (the other was awarded to the Unknown Soldier).

SINGLE-SEAT FIGHTERS

Nieuport 24 and 27

A further improvement to the aerodynamics of the Nieuport Scout resulted in a new, more streamlined fuselage shape and distinctive rounded tail surfaces, though negligible increases in engine power meant the new Nieuport possessed a similar performance to its predecessor.

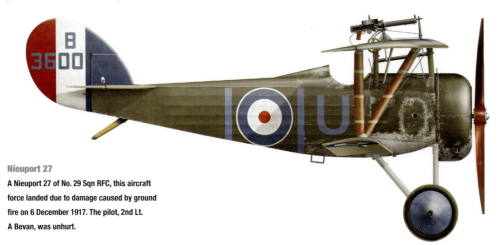

Nieuport 27
A Nieuport 27 of No. 29 Sqn RFC, this aircraft force landed due to damage caused by ground fire on 6 December 1917. The pilot, 2nd Lt. A Bevan, was unhurt.

The Nieuport 24 utilized the same fuselage as the Nieuport 17bis but mated this to new flying surfaces of improved form with a different aerofoil section and distinctive, rounded wingtips to reduce drag. The tail unit was also redesigned into a rounded form, constructed out of moulded plywood, though production delays meant that many Nieuport 24s would utilize the standard Nieuport 17 tail unit and were known as the Nieuport 24bis. First flown in early 1917 (the exact date is now unknown), the Nieuport 24 was designed in response to the appearance of the SPAD VII as an attempt to keep the basic Nieuport sesquiplane design competitive but was, at best, only partially successful. Nonetheless, delays in the supply of more capable fighters in both France and the UK saw both the Nieuport 24 and later Nie 27 built and operated in large numbers. Armament of both types consisted of a single synchronized Vickers gun on the fuselage decking, though British machines were also fitted with an overwing Lewis gun on a Foster mount.

Initial deliveries
Deliveries of the Nieuport 24 to French operational squadrons began in the summer of 1917, and although the SPAD was preferred, in November Nieuport Scouts still made up just under half of all French fighter types at the front. Deliveries to British units began at approximately the same time as their French counterparts, and Nieuport 24 deliveries were regarded as a top priority owing to delays in S.E.5 production. Five RFC squadrons would operate the Nie 24, but even greater use was made of its successor, the Nieuport 27. Little changed from the earlier model and virtually identical in external appearance (and performance), the

Nieuport 27
Weight (Maximum take-off): 535kg (1179lb)
Dimensions: Length 5.87m (19ft 3in), Wingspan 8.21m (26ft 11in), Height 2.4m (7ft 10in)
Powerplant: one 97kW (130hp) Le Rhône 9JB nine-cylinder air-cooled rotary piston engine
Maximum speed: 70km/h (110mph)
Range: 250km (160 miles)
Ceiling: 6850m (22,470ft)
Crew: one
Armament: one 7.7mm (0.303in) Vickers machine gun and on British aircraft one 7.7mm (0.303in) Lewis optionally mounted above the top wing

Nieuport 27 would persist in frontline service into 1918, with two British squadrons operating the type after the formation of the RAF in April 1918, by which time the type had largely been transferred to less demanding theatres synch as Palestine. Ultimately, nine British fighter squadrons used the Nie 27 as their primary equipment before the aircraft switched to training and trial work.

20

SINGLE-SEAT FIGHTERS

Extensive usage

By the time the last of the classic Nieuport scouts made their appearance in mid-1917, the nature of air combat over the Western Front had changed, with the emphasis shifting to high speed and altitude performance rather than outright manoeuvrability. Although the later Nieuport Scouts did possess better speed performance than earlier models, they could not compete with such aircraft as the SPAD. By contrast, their handling was not as pleasant as it had been, with heavy ailerons and somewhat sluggish control in turns, which did not endear them to pilots in quite the same way as the universally praised Nieuport 17. Nonetheless, delays in the supply of more capable fighters saw both the Nieuport 24 and the later 27 built and operated in large numbers, and some pilots preferred the nimble Nieuports to the fast but comparatively unmanoeuvrable SPADs, notably French ace Charles Nungesser, who retained a Nieuport for his personal use even though the rest of his squadron had re-equipped with SPADs. The end of the war saw Nieuports continue serving with many air forces, and the last known operational examples were retired in Uruguay in 1931.

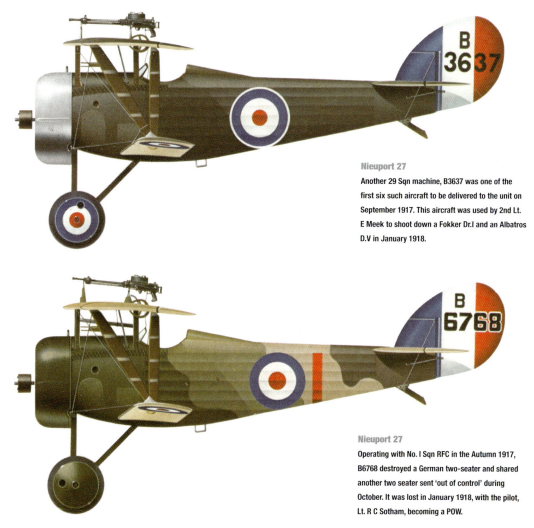

Nieuport 27
Another 29 Sqn machine, B3637 was one of the first six such aircraft to be delivered to the unit on September 1917. This aircraft was used by 2nd Lt. E Meek to shoot down a Fokker Dr.I and an Albatros D.V in January 1918.

Nieuport 27
Operating with No. I Sqn RFC in the Autumn 1917, B6768 destroyed a German two-seater and shared another two seater sent 'out of control' during October. It was lost in January 1918, with the pilot, Lt. R C Sotham, becoming a POW.

21

SINGLE-SEAT FIGHTERS

Vickers FB.19

Although derived from a promising design with excellent speed performance, the FB.19 proved disappointing in British service but enjoyed greater success in Russian hands.

Nicknamed the Bullet, the FB.19 was the production development of the E.S.1 (Experimental Scout 1), first flown in August 1915, which had demonstrated an extremely high top speed of 190km/h (118mph). Fitted with Vickers' own Challenger gun synchronization system, only three were built, and though criticized for their poor visibility and capricious landing behaviour, operational tests suggested that a developed version had a promising future. Unfortunately, this did not transpire to be the case. The production F.B.19 possessed similarly poor visibility to its predecessor – the clearest view was claimed to be directly upwards, and the speed of the new aircraft was no longer particularly impressive, being broadly comparable with its contemporaries. Unpopular with pilots, six RFC squadrons would fly examples of the F.B.19, but none were ever completely equipped with the type. After brief service over the Western Front, around 25 were sent to the less demanding theatres in the Middle East, Palestine and Macedonia. A few Bullets were retained for Home Defence and training, but by the end of 1917, the British career of the F.B.19 was over.

Russian service

Despite this inauspicious career in British hands, the F.B.19 enjoyed considerably greater success in Russia, where it was known as the 'Vickers Bullitt'. Russian examples were usually equipped with a more powerful 130hp Clerget, and in this form, the aircraft boasted a top speed of around 200km/h (124mph) – slightly better than the highly regarded (and notably fast) SPAD S.VII. Approximately 30 aircraft (exact figures are now unknown) were taken into Russian service and were highly regarded by their pilots, including

Vickers FB.19
Weight (Maximum take-off): 674kg (1485lb)
Dimensions: Length 5.54m (18ft 2in), Wingspan 7.32m (24ft), Height 2.51m (8ft 3in)
Powerplant: one 75kW (100hp) Gnome Monosoupape nine-cylinder air-cooled rotary piston engine
Maximum speed: 164km/h (102mph)
Endurance: 2 hours 45 minutes
Ceiling: 5300m (17,500ft)
Crew: one
Armament: one 7.7mm (0.303in) Lewis machine gun fixed forward firing in nose

Imperial Russian ace Grigory Suk, who achieved two of his nine victories with the type. After 1917, the F.B.19 was used by both sides during the Russian Civil War, and some aircraft remained in Soviet service until 1924.

Vickers FB.19

Although little used by its country of origin, a few FB.19s did see action with British forces, notably in Macedonia. A5221 is a later production machine by which time a pronounced stagger had been added to the wings.

22

SINGLE-SEAT FIGHTERS

Sopwith Pup

Famed for its delightful handling, the Pup was the first of Sopwith's 'flying zoo' of aircraft named after animals. Arguably the first unequivocally successful British single-seat fighter, the Pup was built in large numbers and cemented Sopwith's reputation as a combat aircraft producer.

Sopwith Pup
Training aircraft were permitted far more dramatic colour schemes than those on active duty. This impressively striped Pup served with the School of Special Flying, Gosport in the summer of 1917.

Officially named the Sopwith Scout, though almost universally referred to as the Pup (because it was regarded as the 'pup' of the two-seat 1½ Strutter), Sopwith's first foray into single-seat fighter design was spectacularly successful. Derived from a personal runabout aircraft built for company test pilot Harry Hawker, featuring lateral control by ailerons rather than wing-warping and a more powerful engine, the Pup flew for the first time on 9 February 1916. A production order for the RNAS was placed shortly after the prototype completed its service tests with the Navy at Upavon, and the first production aircraft began to be received in August. Sopwith was heavily committed to the 1½ Strutter programme in mid-1916, so deliveries were initially very slow. When the RFC also ordered a large quantity of Pups, it became clear that subcontractors would be required, and ultimately only 96 of the 1796 Pups built were actually built by Sopwith. The vast majority were built by the Standard Motor Company and Whitehead aircraft. The Pup was the first British single-seater equipped with a synchronized machine gun, the single Vickers gun utilizing the same Sopwith-Kauser synchronizer as the 1½ Strutter.

Early use

The first Pups reached the Western Front, with 8 Squadron RNAS, in October 1916 and immediately proved successful. The first RFC Pup squadron, No. 54, arrived at the front in December. With a lightweight structure and generous wing area, the Pup was notably agile and demonstrated an excellent rate of climb, outclassing German fighters then in use, such as the Albatros D.I and D.II as well as the Halberstadts and Fokkers. Popular with pilots due to its easy flying characteristics, it was said that the Pup could turn a complete circle twice before an Albatros had even completed one. The Pup's ascendency at the front was short-lived, however, the frenetic pace of aircraft development at this time saw superior German machines

Sopwith Pup
Weight (Maximum take-off): 556kg (1225lb)
Dimensions: Length 5.89m (19ft 4in), Wingspan 8.08m (26ft 6in), Height 2.87m (9ft 5in)
Powerplant: one 60kW (80hp) Le Rhône 9C nine-cylinder air-cooled rotary piston engine
Maximum speed: 180km/h (112mph)
Range: 542km (337 miles)
Ceiling: 5300m (17,500ft)
Crew: one
Armament: one 7.7mm (0.303in) Vickers machine gun fixed firing forward on upper forward fuselage

SINGLE-SEAT FIGHTERS

Beardmore-built Pup N6438, named 'Excuse Me!' was photographed after making its fifth landing on HMS *Furious* during trials in 1917. Skid landing gear initially seemed more promising than wheels for carrier operations.

appear in the spring of 1917, and the Pup was replaced by Sopwith Triplanes in RNAS squadrons, whilst RFC units had to soldier on with it until it could be replaced by the Camel at the end of 1917. Its excellent flying qualities saw it utilized as an advanced trainer long after it left the frontline, and numerous examples were retained as personal aircraft and squadron hacks. It was even developed into a civilian sporting aircraft, the Sopwith Dove, of which ten were built in 1919.

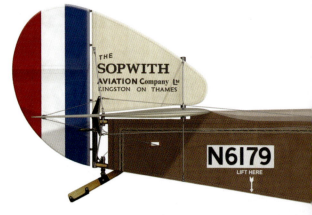

Naval role

The Pup also enjoyed a secondary career as a naval aircraft. On 2 August 1917, a Pup became the first aircraft to land on a moving ship at sea, and the Pup pioneered operations aboard the first extemporized aircraft carriers as well as flying off platforms mounted on gun turrets on cruisers and battleships. On 21 August 1917, a Pup flown from a platform on the cruiser HMS *Yarmouth* shot down the Zeppelin L 23 off the Danish coast, the first air-to-air interception made by a shipborne aircraft. Pups were also used by two Home Defence squadrons formed specifically to combat the Gotha raids on London. The aircraft used for this purpose utilized a more powerful 75kW (100hp) Gnome Monosoupape engine to increase their rate of climb and were easily distinguished by the extra cooling holes cut in the cowling required by the new engine. In addition to their British use, Pups also served in the fighter role with Belgium and Russia, and the type was used as a pioneer carrier aircraft with the US.

Sopwith Pup
Weight (Maximum take-off): 556kg (1225lb)
Dimensions: Length 5.89m (19ft 4in), Wingspan 8.08m (26ft 6in), Height 2.87m (9ft 5in)
Powerplant: one 60kW (80hp) Le Rhône 9C nine-cylinder air-cooled rotary piston engine
Maximum speed: 180km/h (112mph)
Range: 542km (337 miles)
Ceiling: 5300m (17,500ft)
Crew: one
Armament: one 7.7mm (0.303in) Vickers machine gun fixed firing forward on upper forward fuselage

SINGLE-SEAT FIGHTERS

Sopwith Pup
One of a batch of late production Pups built by the Standard Motor company during 1917 and 1918. By the time the aircraft had been superseded at the front and many of these pups were delivered straight into storage.

Sopwith Pup
Flying with 'B' Flight of No. 3(N) Sqn in early 1917, 'Baby Mine' was used by future 17 victory Canadian ace Alfred Carter to shoot down two Albatros D.IIIs on 23 April and a third on the 29th.

SINGLE-SEAT FIGHTERS

Airco DH.5

A distinctive design with its backwards staggered wings, the DH.5 was subject to delays, and by the time it appeared at the front, its performance was inadequate. In service, it did not prove popular, and its operational life was brief.

Designed by Geoffrey de Havilland as a replacement for the obsolescent DH.2, the DH.5 was intended to combine the excellent visibility of pusher aircraft with the greater performance potential of the tractor layout. As a result, the aircraft featured a backwards wing stagger, with the upper plane mounted behind the pilot's head allowing an unimpeded view in the upper forward hemisphere. First flown in August 1916, the aircraft was subject to a major redesign of the rear fuselage, a completely revised fuel system and various other smaller modifications, all of which contributed to a delayed service entry for the new machine. The first production machine issued to the RFC was taken on strength with 24 Squadron in May 1917, but production difficulties resulted in very slow deliveries.

Brief service roles
In service, the DH.5's performance proved inferior to the earlier Sopwith Pup, and whilst the backward staggered wings did indeed confer excellent forward vision on the new aircraft, the upper wing resulted in a blind spot above and to the rear, exactly the direction from which an attacking fighter would tend to approach. Although boasting good handling and decent manoeuvrability as well as great structural strength, the DH.5 tended to lose height in manoeuvring combat, and its ceiling was poor.

With better fighter aircraft such as the SE.5 and Camel already available, few RFC squadrons made use of the type, though the DH.5 did form the initial equipment of the Australian Flying Corps' first fighter squadron. Eventually, the aircraft found a niche of sorts as a relatively effective ground attack aircraft due to its good forward visibility and sturdy construction, but even in this role, its service life proved brief, with the last frontline DH.5s being replaced by the S.E.5a in January 1918.

Airco DH.5

A presentation aircraft, paid for by the 'Women of New South Wales', A9242 was appropriately used by No. 2 Sqn Australian Flying Corps, though to avoid confusion with the British No. 2 Sqn, the unit was designated No. 68 Squadron RFC.

Airco DH.5

Weight (Maximum take-off): 677kg (1492lb)
Dimensions: Length 6.71m (22ft), Wingspan 7.82m (25ft 8in), Height 2.78m (9ft 2in)
Powerplant: one 82kW (110hp) Le Rhône 9J nine-cylinder air-cooled rotary piston engine
Maximum speed: 164km/h (102mph)
Range: 322km (200 miles)
Ceiling: 4900m (16,000ft)
Crew: one
Armament: one 7.7mm (0.303in) Vickers machine gun fixed firing forward on upper fuselage nose decking

SINGLE-SEAT FIGHTERS

Royal Aircraft Factory F.E.8

A contemporary of the better-known DH.2, the F.E.8's service entry was delayed by several months, and once it reached the front, it was no longer competitive with the latest German fighters.

Designed by John Kenworthy, who was later part of the team that developed the superlative S.E.5a, the F.E.8 utilized the same pusher layout as the DH.2 due to the absence of a reliable means to fire through the propeller disc. First flying as early as September 1915, a mere two months after the DH.2, modifications deemed necessary to increase fuel capacity delayed the appearance of the F.E.8 at the front and the first of two units to be wholly equipped with the type, 40 Squadron, only became operational during June 1916.

Poor performance

Initial operational experience was moderately successful, but the F.E.8 struggled to deal with the superior Albatros fighters that appeared towards the end of 1916. The F.E.8 featured an all-metal nacelle of superior streamlined shape to that of the DH.2, but the inherent drag of its pusher design with the mass of struts and wires required to support the tail inevitably meant the aircraft would be slower than an equivalent fighter of conventional layout. The Albatros was faster, much more powerful, and twice as heavily armed as the F.E.8, and its superiority was emphasized in no uncertain terms on 9 March 1917 when nine F.E.8s of 40 Squadron were engaged by five Albatros D.IIIs led by Manfred von Richthofen. Four F.E.8s were shot down, four badly damaged, and the ninth caught fire on landing. 40 Squadron was swiftly re-equipped with Nieuport 17s, but 41 Squadron kept their F.E.8s until July 1917, flying ground attack missions during the Battle of Messines, by which time they were the last single-seat pusher fighters in France.

Royal Aircraft Factory F.E.8
Weight (Maximum take-off): 611kg (1346lb)
Dimensions: Length 7.01m (23ft), Wingspan 9.6m (31ft 6in), Height 2.79m (9ft 2in)
Powerplant: one 75kW (100hp) Gnome Monosoupape B-2 nine-cylinder air-cooled rotary piston engine
Maximum speed: 151km/h (94mph)
Endurance: 2 hours 30 minutes
Ceiling: 4400m (14,500ft)
Crew: one
Armament: one 7.7mm (0.303in) Lewis machine gun fixed forward firing in nose

RAF FE.8

Built by the Darracq Motor Engineering company in Fulham, London, and delivered to No. 40 Sqn RFC in August 1916, this aircraft survived until it was accidentally destroyed in a fire on the ground at the end of January 1917.

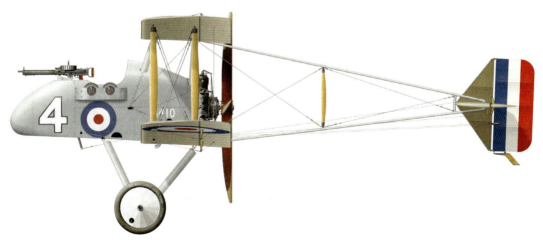

SINGLE-SEAT FIGHTERS

Bristol M.1

The only British-designed monoplane combat aircraft to see active service during World War I, the M1C possessed considerable promise but ultimately served only in secondary theatres.

Bristol M.1C
Built in November 1917 and based at No. 1 School of Aerial Fighting at Turnberry in Scotland during 1918, this M.1C featured a striking high-visibility finish. Featuring high performance and excellent handling, the M.1C was highly prized by instructors.

Designed and built as a private venture by the Bristol Aircraft Company, the M.1 represented the state of the art in flight as envisioned by chief designer Frank Barnwell. Featuring a monoplane configuration for low drag, particular care was paid to minimizing drag, resulting in the M.1's unusually sleek appearance compared to its contemporaries. The first example, designated the M.1A, flew for the first time in July 1916 and quickly demonstrated excellent performance with a speed comfortably in excess of any other fighter, reportedly achieving 212km/h (132mph). Official service tests demonstrated that the aircraft was fast and stable, though pilots criticized the downward vision, which was impaired by the wing, and noted that the aircraft was not easy to land. Nonetheless, the overall impression was very good, and the War Office ordered another four airframes for evaluation, designated M.1B.

Missed opportunity

However, for reasons that are unclear, the further development of the M.1 was marked by official indifference and a general lack of urgency. Despite a favourable evaluation, the M.1 was ordered into production only in August 1917 as the M.1C, but forbidden for use on the Western Front, the official reason being that the landing speed was too high for small French airfields. Given that the stalling speed (79km/h; 49mph) was almost exactly the same as the widely used Sopwith Camel (77km/h; 48mph), it has long been speculated that the Bristol M.1C was the victim of an institutional mistrust of monoplane designs. As a result, the M.1C saw action only in the Balkans and Middle East, where it

Bristol M.1
Weight (Maximum take-off): 611kg (1348lb)
Dimensions: Length 6.22m (20ft 5in), Wingspan 9.37m (30ft 9in), Height 2.36m (7ft 9in)
Powerplant: one 82kW (110hp) Le Rhône 9J nine-cylinder air-cooled rotary piston engine
Maximum speed: 210km/h (132mph)
Range: 350km (217 miles)
Ceiling: 6100m (20,000ft)
Crew: one
Armament: one 7.7mm (0.303in) Vickers machine gun fixed firing forward on upper fuselage nose decking

was very highly regarded despite only 33 seeing operational service. A single pilot, Captain Frederick Dudley Travers achieved five victories (of a total of nine) with the M.1C, including one over the Fokker D.VII, arguably the finest fighter of the war. One hundred and thirty were built in total, with most serving in training units.

28

SINGLE-SEAT FIGHTERS

Sopwith Triplane

Operated solely by the RNAS, the Sopwith Triplane's outstanding combat performance delivered a reputation and effect that starkly contrasted with the modest production run of this remarkable aircraft.

Sopwith Triplane

'Black Maria' was Raymond Collishaw's aircraft when he commanded the Canadian manned 'Black Flight' of No. 10(N) Sqn RNAS. The flight claimed 87 aircraft downed between May and July 1917 garnering them considerable notoriety amongst their German foes.

Developed as a private venture supervised by Sopwith's chief designer Herbert Smith, Sopwith's triplane was, in most regards, a conventional aircraft. Its fuselage was virtually identical to the earlier Pup, and the aircraft was very simple in its construction. The triplane wing arrangement, however, was radical, and the Sopwith was the world's first military triplane to see service. The use of three narrow chord wings was intended primarily to maximize visibility from the cockpit whilst maintaining a respectable wing area within relatively compact dimensions: the Triplane's wingspan was the same as the Pup, and although its total wing area was very slightly smaller, it was noted for its exceptional manoeuvrability and rate of climb.

Sopwith Triplane
Weight (Maximum take-off): 699kg (1541lb)
Dimensions: Length 5.74m (18ft 10in), Wingspan 8.08m (26ft 6in), Height 3.2m (10ft 6in)
Powerplant: one 97kW (130hp) Clerget 9B 9-cylinder air-cooled rotary piston engine
Maximum speed: 188km/h (117mph)
Range: 517km (320 miles)
Ceiling: 6200m (20,500ft)
Crew: one
Armament: one 7.7mm (0.303in) Vickers machine gun fixed firing forward on fuselage decking

One of just three Triplanes built by Oakley & Co Ltd of Ilford, N5912 is also one of only two original airframes to survive to the present day and is currently in the collection of the RAF Museum.

29

SINGLE-SEAT FIGHTERS

First flight

The Triplane was flown for the first time by Harry Hawker on 28 May 1916 and immediately demonstrated its potential when three minutes after take-off, Hawker looped the prototype three times in succession. This aircraft was sent to France for service evaluation at the front and was in action within a mere 15 minutes of its arrival at Dunkirk on a sortie to intercept enemy aircraft.

The first production aircraft appeared in late 1916, and the first Triplane unit, No. 1 Naval Squadron, arrived in France in December, though it saw little action until the spring of the following year, by which time a further three naval squadrons had formed on the type. In service, the aircraft was highly popular and was nicknamed the 'Tripehound' or simply 'Tripe', proving demonstrably superior to the Albatros D.III, though the German aircraft was faster in a dive and more heavily armed.

The Triplane's obvious quality was also noted by the Germans. In April 1917, Manfred von Richthofen, the 'Red Baron', the most successful World War I ace, remarked that the Triplane was the best Allied fighter at that time, and the Sopwith aircraft provoked what has been described as a 'triplane craze' in Germany; no fewer than 34 triplane fighter prototypes were prepared by German companies in response to it, though only the Fokker Dr.I would see operational service in significant numbers.

'Black Flight'

The Triplane's time at the front was comparatively brief but notably successful, particularly in the hands of 'B' Flight 10 Naval Squadron, known as the 'Black Flight'. Manned by Canadian pilots and commanded by Raymond Collishaw, their aircraft were named Black Maria, Black Prince, Black George, Black Death and Black Sheep, and featured black-painted fins and cowlings. The Black Flight claimed 87 German aircraft in a mere three months, with Collishaw scoring 34 of his 60 victories in the aircraft, becoming the most successful Triplane ace as a result.

Given statistics like these, it seems strange that only 147 Triplanes were ever built and served for less than a year, but the Sopwith Camel started to enter service in June 1917 and offered better performance and agility, more powerful armament as well as sturdier construction. The Triplane was also difficult to maintain at unit level, and all had been withdrawn from the front by the end of 1917.

As well as its use by the RNAS, a single French Triplane squadron was based at Dunkirk and single examples were supplied to Greece and Russia, the latter passing into Soviet service and surviving until the present day.

Sopwith Triplane

N6290, named 'Dixie' served with both No. 1 and No. 8 Sqn In 1988, an exact airworthy replica of this aircraft named 'Dixie II', fitted with an original Clerget 9B engine, was constructed and is pictured above.

SINGLE-SEAT FIGHTERS

SPAD S.VII

One of the most significant fighter aircraft of the Great War, the French SPAD S.VII was sufficiently impressive for it to be taken into service in RFC squadrons and licence production to be undertaken in the United Kingdom.

SPAD S.VII
Serving with No. 23 Squadron RFC, B3504 was last seen on 19 June 1917, "E of Ypres at 2000ft steering west under heavy AA fire in pursuit of enemy aircraft". The pilot, Captain T Davidson was posted missing.

Built by Mann Egerton in Norwich but delivered after the SPAD XIII had become available, B9913 spent the rest of the war being used for various home assignments before being shipped to the US, where it featured in the Oscar-winning 1921 film *Wings*.

SPAD S. VII
Weight (Maximum take-off): 705kg (1554lb)
Dimensions: Length 6.08m (19ft 11in), Wingspan 7.82m (25ft 8in), Height 2.2m (7ft 3in)
Powerplant: one 110kW (150p) Hispano-Suiza 8Aa liquid-cooled V-8 piston engine
Maximum speed: 193km/h (120mph)
Range: 400km (250 miles)
Ceiling: 5500m (18,000ft)
Crew: one
Armament: one 7.7mm (0.303in) Vickers machine gun fixed firing forward in fuselage decking

The appearance in 1915 of a powerful Hispano-Suiza V-8 aero engine, designed by Marc Birkigt, saw French military authorities issue a requirement for a fighter to utilize the new engine and the SPAD S.VII, designed by Louis Béchereau was the outstanding result. Flying for the first time in April 1916, the S.VII was not as manoeuvrable as the Nieuport fighters that preceded it, but the SPAD demonstrated excellent speed performance, rate of climb and diving characteristics. Furthermore, it was an exceptionally sturdy aircraft that could be flown to the limits of its performance with impunity, unlike the dainty Nieuports, which were known to suffer occasional structure failure during flight.

31

SINGLE-SEAT FIGHTERS

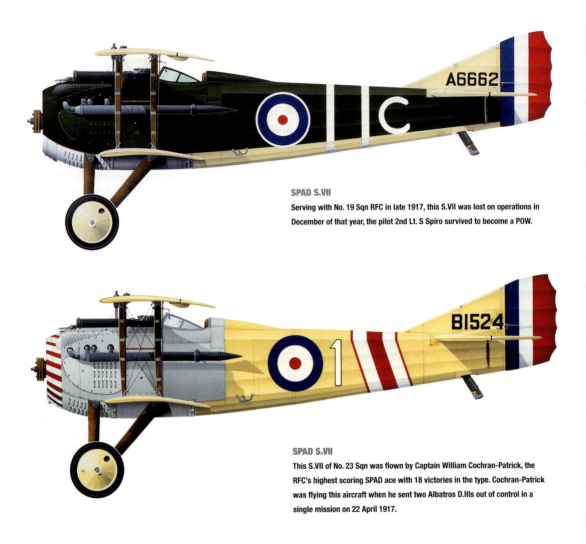

SPAD S.VII
Serving with No. 19 Sqn RFC in late 1917, this S.VII was lost on operations in December of that year, the pilot 2nd Lt. S Spiro survived to become a POW.

SPAD S.VII
This S.VII of No. 23 Sqn was flown by Captain William Cochran-Patrick, the RFC's highest scoring SPAD ace with 18 victories in the type. Cochran-Patrick was flying this aircraft when he sent two Albatros D.IIIs out of control in a single mission on 22 April 1917.

On the front

Thousands of S.VIIs would see service with France, and ultimately over twenty nations would operate the superlative French fighter. The RFC was the first foreign air arm to take the SPAD into action, though only two squadrons would operate it over the Western Front, and a third S.VII-equipped unit flew the aircraft in Mesopotamia. It quickly became clear that French production was insufficient to supply both nations' requirements, so arrangements were made to produce the aircraft under licence at the coachbuilding company Mann Egerton, and ultimately 220 SPAD S.VIIs would be built in Britain.

Unfortunately, it rapidly became clear that British-built SPADs were significantly inferior to their French counterparts (problems including poor fabric sewing, weak tailskids and ineffective radiators) and as a result were only used for training and in the less demanding Middle East theatre, those units operating over the Western Front were equipped exclusively with French-built examples.

In service, the S.VII proved effective and popular until both SPAD-equipped units re-equipped with more modern aircraft at the end of 1917.

SINGLE-SEAT FIGHTERS

Sopwith Camel

Likely the most agile aircraft produced by any nation during the conflict, the Sopwith Camel became the best-known British aircraft of World War I. Although highly successful, it possessed handling traits that regularly proved fatal to the inexperienced.

Designed by Herbert Smith in response to the appearance of German scouts, especially the Albatros D.III, that were proving superior to the Sopwith Pup and contemporary Nieuport 17, the Sopwith F.1 made its maiden flight on 22 November 1916. Initially referred to as the 'Big Pup', the new Sopwith fighter was larger and more powerful, a range of engines from 75kW (100hp) to 120kW (160hp) were utilized on production machines, and for the first time on a British aircraft, featured two synchronized Vickers machine guns. The guns themselves were covered within a metal 'hump' to prevent them from freezing at high altitude, and this is supposedly the origin of the 'Camel' nickname, which, like the Pup before it, was only ever unofficial but became totally ubiquitous. Although of conventional design and construction for its era, the Camel featured a completely horizontal top wing with no dihedral to make mass production simpler, and squeezed pilot, guns and fuel tank (some 90 per cent of the aircraft's weight) into the first 2.1m (7ft) of the fuselage.

The latter feature conferred outstanding manoeuvrability on the aircraft but also led to its tricky handling characteristics, exacerbated by the gyroscopic effect of the spinning rotary engine and the light and sensitive controls. This effect could be used to make incredibly quick turns to the right, but left-hand turns against the rotation of the engine were much slower. Camel pilots found that if they wished to turn directly left it was quicker to kick the rudder to the right and execute a 270° turn rather than perform a conventional 90° left-hand turn.

Sopwith F.1 Camel
Weight (Maximum take-off): 659kg (1453lb)
Dimensions: Length 5.72m (18ft 9in), Wingspan 8.53m (28ft), Height 2.59m (8ft 6in)
Powerplant: one 97kW (130hp) Clerget 9B nine-cylinder air-cooled rotary piston engine
Maximum speed: 182km/h (113mph)
Range: 480km (300 miles)
Ceiling: 5800m (19,000ft)
Crew: one
Armament: two 7.7mm (0.303in) Vickers machine guns fixed firing forward in fuselage decking

First victory
The first unit to convert to the new Sopwith was No.4 Squadron RNAS, which flew their first patrol and scored the Camel's first victory, on 7 July 1917. Two more naval units and 70. Squadron RFC also became operational on the

Sopwith Camel
Canadian Captain Lloyd Breadner flew this distinctive Camel with No. 3 Sqn RNAS. As well as the rising sun motif on fin and elevators, the aircraft also sported King of Diamonds playing cards on top of the lower wings, the badge of the Canadian Expeditionary Force behind the cockpit and two huge white circles on the top wing.

33

SINGLE-SEAT FIGHTERS

Sopwith Camel
Featuring a portrait of the hugely popular comedian George Robey on its fin (a cut out from a poster advertising the revue 'Zig Zag' doped onto the fin), B3881 served with 'A' Flight of No. 9(N) Sqn RNAS.

type before the end of the month. By February 1918, 13 squadrons were equipped with Camels and along with the SPAD XIII and S.E.5a, the Camel regained air supremacy for the Allies over the Western Front. The Camel's speed performance was approximately equivalent to that of the Albatros D.III and D.V, and its famed manoeuvrability was superior to any contemporary.

Record kills
Ultimately, the Camel would be credited with shooting down 1294 enemy aircraft, more than any other Allied fighter of World War I. The most successful individual airframe in RAF history was the Sopwith Camel B6313, utilized by Major William Barker to shoot down 46 balloons and aircraft. Despite these successes, however, the Camel was initially quite an unpopular aircraft. It was difficult and tiring to fly, possessed a vicious stall and was notoriously tricky to handle on take-off in particular: the aircraft was tail-heavy at medium and low altitude, and if the fuel tank was full, the centre of gravity was pushed dangerously aft, which could lead to a stall directly after lifting off, often with fatal results.

To further complicate the issue, the torque generated by the engine and propeller at full throttle was barely within the capability of the rudder to control and as a result, the aircraft was susceptible to uncontrollably veering to the right. The situation was serious enough that a two-seat version, known as the 'Training Camel', was developed and issued to flying schools, which helped to alleviate the problem somewhat, but the Camel retained its fearsome reputation for being simultaneously both dangerous and effective.

Pilots morbidly joked that the Sopwith fighter offered the choice between "a wooden cross, the Red Cross, or a Victoria Cross", and of the 420 Camel pilots that would lose their lives in combat, a further 380 were killed in training accidents. In the hands of an experienced pilot, of course, the very same qualities that rendered the Camel so dangerous to the tyro conferred upon it the outstanding combat performance for which it became famed.

SINGLE-SEAT FIGHTERS

This photograph is believed to depict William Barker flying B6313, the most successful single British fighter airframe, in which Barker claimed 46 aircraft and balloons between September 1917 and September 1918.

RNAS

Like many Sopwith products of World War I, the Camel's development was initially undertaken primarily for use by the RNAS, and whilst the aircraft was cementing its reputation over the Western Front, further work to more thoroughly integrate the aircraft for naval use resulted in the Sopwith 2F.1 'Ship's Camel'. This variant featured a shortened wingspan and two-piece fuselage to aid in storage aboard Royal Naval vessels as well as steel cabane struts and lifting points on the upper wing centre section to allow the aircraft to be hoisted aboard by crane. Flotation bags were mounted in the fuselage to assist in the event of ditching at sea, and wireless equipment was sometimes fitted to allow the aircraft to undertake gunnery spotting duties. With an overwing Lewis gun replacing one of the fuselage-mounted Vickers, 276 Sopwith 2F.1 Camels were built, and most saw service at sea, taking off from platforms atop gun turrets on cruisers and battleships or from towed lighters. Ship's Camels also served from the pioneer aircraft carrier HMS *Furious*, and on 19 July 1918, seven aircraft each carrying launched from this vessel made history by performing the first attack in history by aircraft

Sopwith Camel
Major Donald Maclaren, who would become the most successful Camel pilot with 54 victories in total, flew this aircraft whilst commanding 46 Squadron RAF. He achieved his last nine victories with this machine in September and October 1918.

35

SINGLE-SEAT FIGHTERS

Sopwith 2F.1 Ship's Camel
2F.1 Ship's Camel N6818 was finished in this remarkable scheme and flown by Major WG Moore. The arresting colours were applied as a visibility aid should the aircraft have to ditch in the sea, a common occurrence at the time.

from an aircraft carrier, a bombing mission targeting the Imperial German Navy airship base at Tønder, then part of Germany but now in Denmark. The aircraft destroyed Zeppelins L 54, L 60 and a captive balloon in their hangars.

The Camel Comic

Another important 'first' was achieved by the Camel in the field of nocturnal fighting. On the night of 18 December 1917, Gilbert Murlis Green shot down a Gotha G.IV, despite the flash of the guns temporarily blinding him, becoming the first pilot of any nation to successfully intercept an enemy aeroplane by night. The Camel's effectiveness as a night fighter was improved when two Lewis guns firing over the top wing, outside the pilot's field of vision, replaced the standard fuselage-mounted Vickers guns. Furthermore, the cockpit was moved rearwards so the pilot could pull the guns back and replace the ammunition drums, which also allowed for the weapons to be fired upwards. The

Sopwith F.1 Camel
Weight (Maximum take-off): 659kg (1453lb)
Dimensions: Length 5.72m (18ft 9in), Wingspan 8.53m (28ft), Height 2.59m (8ft 6in)
Powerplant: one 97kW (130hp) Clerget 9B nine-cylinder air-cooled rotary piston engine
Maximum speed: 182km/h (113mph)
Range: 480km (300 miles)
Ceiling: 5800m (19,000ft)
Crew: one
Armament: two 7.7mm (0.303in) Vickers machine guns fixed firing forward in fuselage decking

SINGLE-SEAT FIGHTERS

changes were sufficient to give this Camel variant an apparently 'comical' appearance compared to the standard version, leading to it being known as the Camel 'Comic', and it became the standard British night fighter during 1918. Murlis Green took command of No. 151 squadron, a dedicated nocturnal unit, which operated Comic Camels over Europe to great effect. From June 1918 until the armistice, the squadron shot down 26 bombers and suffered no casualties, as well as beginning to undertake what would come to be known as night intruder operations in World War II. On the night of 21/22 August, for example, 151 sqn bombed aerodromes at Moslains and Offoy, and a German aircraft was shot down in flames near Arras. Such was the success of these operations that a further four Camel squadrons were earmarked for night use over France but only one saw brief service before the armistice.

Final years

By the time the Camel was undertaking such nocturnal sorties, it was beginning to become obsolescent as a standard fighter by day, its speed was inadequate, and altitude performance was insufficient to effectively combat the latest German fighters, particularly the superlative Fokker D.VII. Though delays in the development of the Snipe saw the Camel soldier on in the air-superiority role until the armistice, the aircraft was increasingly used as a ground attack aircraft during 1918, a role in which it excelled despite the significant losses experienced in these dangerous missions. During the German spring offensive of March 1918, for example, several Camel

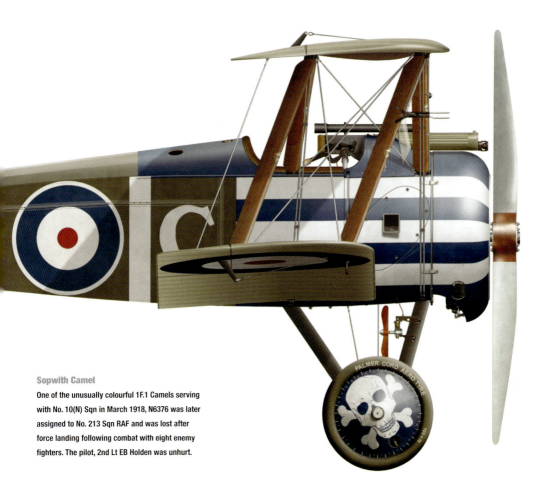

Sopwith Camel
One of the unusually colourful 1F.1 Camels serving with No. 10(N) Sqn in March 1918, N6376 was later assigned to No. 213 Sqn RAF and was lost after force landing following combat with eight enemy fighters. The pilot, 2nd Lt EB Holden was unhurt.

SINGLE-SEAT FIGHTERS

squadrons intensively harassed the advancing German Army. During these missions, Camels flew as low as 150m (500ft) to maintain surprise when strafing ground forces, and much of the British strategy intended to contain the offensive depended upon ground attack aircraft, the majority of which were Camels. Air attacks were observed to produce confusion and panic amongst the advancing German forces, and subsequently, a dedicated ground attack variant was developed, the Sopwith T.F.1, standing for 'Trench Fighter 1' with machine guns angled downwards for maximum effect when strafing, and featuring armour plating for protection. The T.F.1 never entered production, but aspects of the design were incorporated into the Snipe-derived Sopwith T.F.2 Salamander, of which 1400 were ordered, although most were cancelled at the armistice.

Post-war usage

The end of hostilities saw the rapid withdrawal of the Camel from the RAF, though some aircraft would see action again with the RAF and White Russian forces in 1919 and early 1920 during the Russian Civil War. Captured aircraft would subsequently serve the Soviet Union. As well as its major use with British and Commonwealth forces, the Camel was also used in action in significant numbers by Belgium and the US during World War I and in smaller numbers by the Netherlands, Greece, Estonia and Latvia. Both Georgia and Poland operated Camels post-war. In total, 5490 Camels were built.

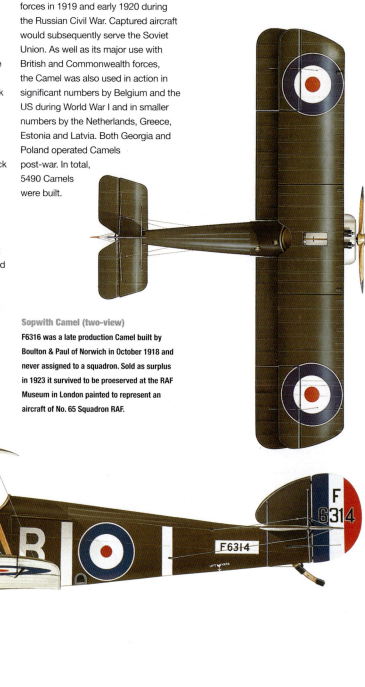

Sopwith Camel (two-view)
F6316 was a late production Camel built by Boulton & Paul of Norwich in October 1918 and never assigned to a squadron. Sold as surplus in 1923 it survived to be preserved at the RAF Museum in London painted to represent an aircraft of No. 65 Squadron RAF.

SINGLE-SEAT FIGHTERS

Royal Aircraft Factory S.E.5 and S.E.5a

Arguably the finest British single-seat fighter to see widespread service during the war, the S.E.5 lacked the outright manoeuvrability of the Camel but complemented the Sopwith fighter to a remarkable degree with its much superior speed and altitude performance.

RAF SE.5

Canadian William Avery Bishop was officially credited with 72 victories, though controversy lingers over the true total as there were no witnesses to over half of them. Bishop flew this strikingly marked S.E.5 with No. 60 Sqn RFC in the summer 0f 1917, the aircraft was subsequently converted to S.E.5a standard and served with 68 Sqn.

Designed by a trio of talented designers, John Kenworthy, Henry Folland (who would later design the famed Gloster Gladiator and Folland Gnat jet trainer), and Major Frank Gooden, who, unusually for this era, was a serving military test pilot of considerable experience, the S.E.5 (standing for 'Scout Experimental 5') was developed specifically to utilize the new French Hispano-Suiza 8 engine, a V-8 unit that developed 112kW (150hp) with the possibility of greater power output in future. Although flown as early as 22 November 1916 (a month to the day before the Camel), the S.E.5 programme was dealt a terrible blow when designer Gooden was killed following wing failure on one of the first prototypes. The wing was redesigned, and ultimately, the S.E.5 would gain a reputation for great structural strength, but time delays were incurred as the problem was solved.

Performance

Unlike most of its peers, the S.E.5 was relatively easy to fly and forgiving resulting in a much better accident rate than contemporary fighters, not least its demanding contemporary, the Camel. Although prone to an unusual amount of adverse yaw, which was easily compensated for, it was generally stable, allowing pilots to open fire from longer ranges than usual with reasonable accuracy.
The mass-produced S.E.5a was the fastest British fighter to become operational during the war, and its great structural strength conferred excellent crashworthiness and survivability on the aircraft – important considerations in a pre-parachute age. Its excellent altitude capability allowed the S.E.5 to meet the much-vaunted Fokker D.VII on roughly equal terms when it began to appear over the Front in mid-1918. Despite the obvious quality of the aircraft, the first S.E.5s were not received with great enthusiasm by the initial unit to operate them, No. 56 Squadron RFC. The main problem, as far as the pilots were concerned, was the unusual design choice selected

Royal Aircraft Factory S.E.5
Weight (Maximum take-off): 878kg (1935lb)
Dimensions: Length 6.38m (20ft 11in), Wingspan 8.51m (27ft 11in), Height 2.87m (9ft 5in)
Powerplant: one 112kW (150hp) Hispano-Suiza water-cooled V8 piston engine
Maximum speed: 196km/h (122mph)
Range: 480km (300 miles)
Ceiling: 5790m (19,000ft)
Crew: one
Armament: one 7.7mm (0.303in) Vickers machine gun in fuselage decking and one 7.7mm (0.303in) Lewis mounted above top wing centre section

39

SINGLE-SEAT FIGHTERS

for the cockpit intended to maximize pilot visibility. This consisted of a seat mounted unusually high in the fuselage coupled with a large celluloid windscreen structure (immediately dubbed 'the greenhouse') to protect the pilot's largely exposed body from the slipstream. The aircraft was also much larger and heavier than the small fighting scouts pilots were generally familiar with, such as the Nieuport 17. 56 Squadron arrived in France in April 1917 but only flew their first missions towards the end of the month once the windscreen had been replaced with a conventional small unit and the seat lowered to a less unusual position - with no obvious effect on visibility, the all-round view from the cockpit often being cited as a strong point of the type by RFC pilots. Initial suspicion gradually gave way to respect as the fine flying qualities of the type became apparent on operations.

Engine issues

More serious was the engine situation, only 79 examples of the basic Hispano-Suiza eight-powered S.E.5 would be produced and only 56 Squadron was ever wholly equipped with the type. Acute problems in engine supply, combined with a lack of engine reliability and the realization that the 112kW engine wasn't powerful enough led to the appearance of the improved S.E.5a during June 1917. The new version featured a 149kW (200hp) Hispano-Suiza 8B, 8Ba or 8Bb and put an end to suggestions that the aircraft was underpowered. Engine supply issues remained, however, and would continue to dog the S.E.5a until the British-manufactured Hispano-Suiza derivative, the Wolseley Viper began to be fitted to the aircraft in late 1917, this power unit also discarded the Hispano-Suiza's troublesome airscrew gearing system, effectively solving the reliability issue.

Royal Aircraft Factory S.E.5a
Weight (Maximum take-off): 902kg (1988lb)
Dimensions: Length 6.38m (20ft 11in), Wingspan 8.1m (26ft 7in), Height 2.9m (9ft 6in)
Powerplant: one 149kW (200hp) Hispano-Suiza 8 or Wolseley Viper water-cooled V8 piston engine
Maximum speed: 222km/h (138mph)
Range: 480km (300 miles)
Ceiling: 5945m (19,500ft)
Crew: one
Armament: one 7.7mm (0.303in) Vickers machine gun in fuselage decking and one 7.7mm (0.303in) Lewis mounted above top wing centre section

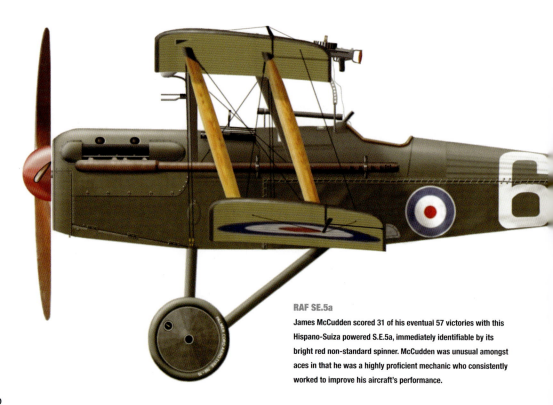

RAF SE.5a
James McCudden scored 31 of his eventual 57 victories with this Hispano-Suiza powered S.E.5a, immediately identifiable by its bright red non-standard spinner. McCudden was unusual amongst aces in that he was a highly proficient mechanic who consistently worked to improve his aircraft's performance.

SINGLE-SEAT FIGHTERS

RAF SE.5a
Roderick Dallas was a 39 victory Australian ace who flew with the RNAS and later RAF. By May 1918 he was CO of No.40 Sqn RAF at Bruay in France. His aircraft was one of a handful of S.E.5as finished in this experimental scheme applied in the field.

Armament
A curious feature of all S.E.5s was the armament arrangement, featuring a single synchronized Vickers gun in the nose and a Lewis gun firing from a Foster mount on the top wing centre section above the propeller arc. The dual gun layout was initially selected due to concerns about the reliability of the Constantinesco-Colley hydraulic synchronization gear (or 'C.C. Gear'), in the event of it failing the pilot could still utilize the unsynchronized Lewis gun which also possessed the advantage of a higher rate of fire. The CC synchronization system ultimately proved to be highly reliable and was used on every subsequent British fighter featuring a synchronized machine gun, but the overwing Lewis also had the advantage of being able to be pulled backwards and down towards the pilot, ostensibly for reloading, though it could also be fired from this position, forwards and upwards, allowing an S.E.5 pilot to approach an enemy aircraft in the blind spot behind and below the tail and destroy it before the unsuspecting crew even knew it was there - a technique used to great effect by ace Albert Ball on both the Nieuport and S.E.5a. For taller pilots however, the Foster mount was a constant menace, placed exactly where it was most likely to hit one's head when climbing into or out of the aircraft.

Most successful pilots
S.E.5a deliveries were slow throughout 1917 and into 1918 but production eventually hit its stride, and by the end of hostilities, 21 British and Commonwealth squadrons were flying the type as well as two USAS units. Many aces flew the type to score some of their victories, including the Canadian 'ace of aces' William 'Billy' Bishop and British top-scorer Edward 'Mick' Mannock who achieved 46 of his 61 credited victories with the S.E.5a.

The most successful S.E.5 pilot of all, however, was the South African Andrew Beauchamp-Proctor who scored 54 victories, all with the S.E.5a. A small man at 1.57m (5ft 2in), Beauchamp-Proctor had to have a raised seat in his aircraft to allow him to see out and blocks fitted to the rudder pedals. Other alterations made in the field to S.E5as included those

41

SINGLE-SEAT FIGHTERS

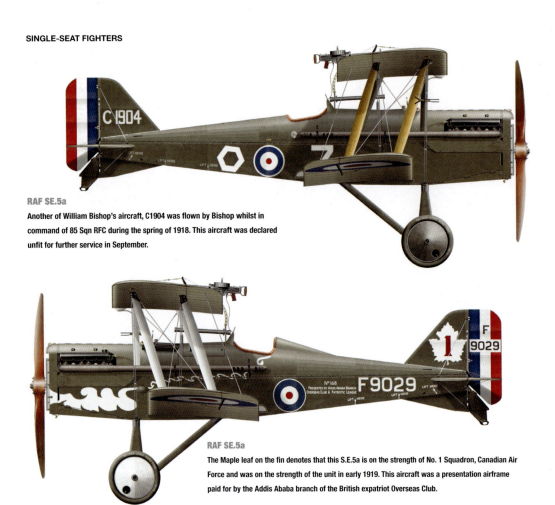

RAF SE.5a
Another of William Bishop's aircraft, C1904 was flown by Bishop whilst in command of 85 Sqn RFC during the spring of 1918. This aircraft was declared unfit for further service in September.

RAF SE.5a
The Maple leaf on the fin denotes that this S.E.5a is on the strength of No. 1 Squadron, Canadian Air Force and was on the strength of the unit in early 1919. This aircraft was a presentation airframe paid for by the Addis Ababa branch of the British expatriot Overseas Club.

of No. 24 Squadron which were rigged with less dihedral in the wings to lessen stability and increase manoeuvrability and 57 victory ace James McCudden's machine which featured shortened exhaust pipes to save weight and improve exhaust scavenging, high compression pistons and a salvaged German propeller spinner. With the engine tuned by McCudden himself, he managed to increase the top speed at altitude by 14km/h (9mph); the spinner, McCudden believed, contributed an increase of 5km/h (3mph) alone.

As well as such 'tinkering' at the unit level, the Royal Aircraft Factory developed the S.E.5b, a variant with sesquiplane wings, and a much more aerodynamic nose featuring a spinner on the propeller and a retractable underslung radiator. Despite its improved looks, the S.E.5b did not offer enough of a performance increase to justify production but the single example built, which flew for the first time in April 1918, survived into the 1920s as a research aircraft. A further development that remained unflown was the T.E.1, a scaled-up two-seat S.E.5a, which was nearing completion when it was cancelled in June 1917, as a result of the success of the Bristol F.2 coupled with ongoing supply issues with Hispano-Suiza engines.

US service
Used almost exclusively during the war by the RFC and RAF, the S.E.5a also served briefly with the US, a single unit, the 25th Aero Squadron, flew their first operational patrol on 10 November 1918; the armistice came into effect the following day. Plans had been made to manufacture large numbers of the S.E.5a in America, with Curtiss receiving orders for around 1000 examples, though only a single Curtiss-built example was completed before the end of hostilities. A further 56 examples of the aircraft were constructed by Eberhart Aeroplane from components that had already been sent over from

SINGLE-SEAT FIGHTERS

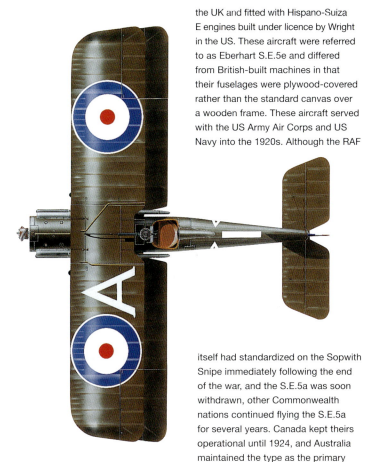

the UK and fitted with Hispano-Suiza E engines built under licence by Wright in the US. These aircraft were referred to as Eberhart S.E.5e and differed from British-built machines in that their fuselages were plywood-covered rather than the standard canvas over a wooden frame. These aircraft served with the US Army Air Corps and US Navy into the 1920s. Although the RAF itself had standardized on the Sopwith Snipe immediately following the end of the war, and the S.E.5a was soon withdrawn, other Commonwealth nations continued flying the S.E.5a for several years. Canada kept theirs operational until 1924, and Australia maintained the type as the primary fighter aircraft of the RAAF until the late 1920s.

Further post-war usage

Other post-war military users were Argentina, Brazil, Chile, Ireland and Poland, and a single example was supplied to the Japanese Navy. A few S.E.5as also found their way into civilian hands, and the type was used by John 'Mad Jack' Savage, a former RAF pilot, to develop skywriting. Savage bought 33 retired S.E.5as and converted them for their new role. Extended asbestos-lagged exhaust pipes were fitted that linked together through a hole cut in the rudder. The smoke-generating oil was stored in front of the cockpit in place of the Vickers machine gun and ammunition.

Designated the 'Savage Wolseley S.E.5a', the first skywriting flight took place in 1922, advertising the Daily Mail at that year's Epsom Derby, and caused a sensation. Savage followed this up by writing 'Hello USA' above New York, reportedly bringing the city to a standstill. Savage's S.E.5as worked hard until the last was withdrawn in 1939 and presented to London's Science Museum. Of the 5205 S.E.5as originally built, six survived to the present day, three of which are ex-Savage skywriting aircraft.

RAF SE.5a (two-view)
The highest scoring British ace of all time, Edward 'Mick' Mannock flew this aircraft, amongst others, whilst serving as a Flight Commander with No. 74. Sqn RFC. Later promoted to command No. 85 Sqn, Mannock eventually achieved 61 official victories.

SINGLE-SEAT FIGHTERS

SPAD S.XIII

Developed from the S.VII to produce an even more formidable fighter, the S.XIII served in very large numbers with France, the US and Italy. The United Kingdom's use of the S.XIII was more modest however, since the type only ever equipping a single RFC squadron.

SPAD S.XIII

Built by Kellner, B6847 retains its factory-applied French camouflage and was used by Captain William Fry to down four of his eleven credited victories. Fry would go on to fly Sopwith Dolphins with 79 Sqn and ultimately survived the war.

With his own S.VII becoming increasingly outclassed by the latest German fighters, Louis Béchereau developed an improved fighter, the S.XIII. Powered by the latest version of the Hispano-Suiza V-8 engine that had proved so effective in the S.VII, Béchereau schemed a new aircraft of similar design but larger and heavier. The new SPAD fighter was developed in two concurrent forms, the S.XII fitted with a 37mm cannon firing through the propeller boss and the more conventional S.XIII with twin Vickers armament. The S.XII proved unpopular, its armament was difficult to use in combat, and only a few were produced, but the S.XIII, by contrast, would become one of the most formidable fighters of the conflict.

French and British usage

Deliveries of the S.XIII to French units began barely a month after its maiden flight on 4 April 1917, and British authorities expressed an early interest in the type. Following the delivery of a single example for testing, the S.XIII's marked superiority over the S.VII led to existing RFC SPAD orders being amended to include 60 of the new type. Ultimately, 57 aircraft would be delivered, all manufactured by Kellner Frères at Billancourt.

British service was to prove relatively limited, with only No. 23 Squadron RFC wholly equipping on the type, receiving their first aircraft in December 1917 to replace the squadron's SPAD S.VIIs. In contrast to those aircraft operated by the French, problems with the engine afflicted the British SPADs throughout their operational use. Nonetheless, the SPAD S.XIII proved modestly successful in RFC/RAF service until 23 Squadron exchanged the French aircraft to re-equip with Sopwith Dolphins in April 1918.

SPAD S.XIII
Weight (Maximum take-off): 857kg (1888lb)
Dimensions: Length 6.25m (20ft 6in), Wingspan 8.25m (27ft 1in), Height 2.60m (8ft 6in)
Powerplant: one 150kW (200hp) Hispano-Suiza 8Ba liquid-cooled V-8 piston engine
Maximum speed: 211 km/h (131 mph)
Endurance: 2 hours
Ceiling: 6800m (22,300ft)
Crew: one
Armament: two 7.7mm (0.303in) Vickers machine guns fixed firing forward in fuselage decking; optional bombload of up to four 11kg (25lb) Cooper bombs

SINGLE-SEAT FIGHTERS

Sopwith 5F.1 Dolphin

Representing a complete departure from Sopwith's previous fighter designs, the Dolphin was unconventional but would prove formidable. Only the poor reliability of its engine prevented it from achieving even greater success.

Sopwith 5F.1 Dolphin
Flown by Canadian ace Gordon Irving, C3799 is still fitted with the upward angled Lewis guns that were generally removed at unit level. Blue denoted B-flight in RAF squadrons and the unusually liberal use of the colour here identifies this as the Flight Commander's aircraft.

Work on the Dolphin began in early 1917 when Herbert Smith started scheming a fighter to utilize the impressive new 150kW (200hp) geared V-8 engine from Hispano-Suiza, in stark contrast to all Sopwith's earlier scouts, which had featured rotary engines. The aircraft that emerged was of a strange, even ungainly appearance, with its back staggered wings and unusual cockpit arrangement with the pilot seated so that his head stuck out above the upper wing centre section. This unconventional design was selected to give the pilot the best possible view, and in the upper hemisphere, there were no impediments to visibility in any direction. A very heavy armament was schemed for the Dolphin, with two Vickers guns conventionally arranged to fire forward, and two Lewis guns fixed firing upwards and forwards and with some degree of flexibility to allow firing at different angles. This would be the most powerfully armed British single seater to enter service until the Gloster Gladiator twenty years later.

Maiden flight
Sopwith's test pilot Harry Hawker flew the Dolphin for the first time on 23 May 1917, and in the following month, the prototype was flown to France for service evaluation, arriving safely despite having been fired upon by Allied anti-aircraft batteries due to its unfamiliar shape.

Reports from service pilots were highly favourable, and the aircraft entered production in October 1917. The first Dolphin unit to become operational was No. 19 Squadron RFC, flying their first patrol with the new fighter on 3 February 1918.

Concerns were raised by pilots regarding the possibility of head and

Sopwith Dolphin
Weight (Maximum take-off): 903kg (1990lb)
Dimensions: Length 6.78m (22ft 3in), Wingspan 9.91m (32ft 6in), Height 2.59m (8ft 6in)
Powerplant: one 150kW (200hp) Hispano-Suiza 8B V-8 water-cooled geared piston engine
Maximum speed: 193.9km/h (120.5mph)
Endurance: 2 hours
Ceiling: 6400m (21,000ft)
Crew: one
Armament: two 7.7mm (0.303in) Vickers machine guns fixed forward firing in nose; up to two 7.7mm (0.303in) Lewis guns semi-flexibly mounted in cockpit firing forward and upward.

neck injuries in the event of the aircraft overturning on the ground, and many Dolphins were fitted with extemporized roll bars, though this fear gradually died away as service use demonstrated that the Dolphin was no more dangerous

45

SINGLE-SEAT FIGHTERS

than any other type. The upward-firing Lewis guns were usually removed as well, as these proved to be difficult to aim and prone to swinging into the pilot's face in high-g manoeuvres. In general, though, the aircraft was very well received, being fast, manoeuvrable and easy to fly. Altitude performance was outstanding when the Hispano-Suiza engine was running properly, and herein lay the Dolphin's only real flaw: its problematic engine.

The HS.8B was initially in short supply, and being a French-built engine, priority was usually given to French aircraft, such as the SPAD XIII, resulting in delays in the deliveries of Dolphins. Compounding the problem was the fact that the HS.8B was unreliable; regular failures of the reduction gearing were experienced, and the engine was persistently hobbled by lubrication problems. Supply problems were eased when the French firm Emile Mayen began supplying engines on a direct order placed by the British Admiralty, but reliability issues remained.

Development of the Dolphin Mk.III with an ungeared engine bid fair to

Sopwith 5F.1 Dolphin serial no. D5263 sits in a field.

solve the problems, but this only entered production in October 1918, and none entered service.

Mk.II

Nonetheless, when the engine was working properly, the Dolphin was arguably the finest British fighter in the sky, and the most successful Dolphin pilot was the American Francis Gillet, who achieved 20 victories with the type. The Dolphin Mk.II that was developed and built by the French firm SACA featured a 220kW (300hp) direct-drive Hispano-Suiza 8F engine and could achieve 225km/h (140mph) and an altitude of 8047m (26,400ft). Thousands were on order for French and US service but only a few were delivered before the Armistice.

In total, 2072 Dolphins Mk.Is were constructed.

Sopwith 5F.1 Dolphin

C4131 was used by 79 Sqn American pilot Frederic Ives to down four of his eventual 12 victories, including two Albatros D.Vs and a Fokker Dr.I during the course of one mission in June 1918. Ives would go on to fight on the Republican side in the Spanish Civil War.

SINGLE-SEAT FIGHTERS

Sopwith Snipe

Sopwith's replacement for its hugely successful Camel, the Snipe was operational for less than two months before the war ended but was built in large numbers and served in the RAF into the 1920s.

Flown for the first time in October 1917, the Snipe delivered a usefully increased maximum speed compared to the Camel and possessed much-improved visibility from the cockpit. The aircraft benefitted from a considerably stronger airframe, and crucially, although somewhat heavier than the Camel, it was much easier to fly. Following successful evaluation after a somewhat protracted development, the first RAF unit to equip on the Snipe, No. 43 Squadron, conducted its first operational patrol on 24 September 1918 but saw comparatively little action before the armistice. By contrast, the Australian No. 4 Squadron re-equipped with the Snipe during October and scored 15 victories in a four-day period towards the end of that month. The Snipe was also the sole Allied aircraft in one of the most famous engagements of the war when the Canadian Major William Barker of 201 Squadron RAF single-handedly fought a formation of at least 15 Fokker D.VIIs, shooting down three. This action was witnessed by hundreds of troops on the ground and resulted in Barker being awarded the Victoria Cross, Britain's highest award for bravery.

Cheap to manufacture

Orders for 4500 Snipes had been placed by the armistice, but most of these were subsequently cancelled, and ultimately 497 Snipes were built. A further 210 examples were constructed of an armoured ground-attack variant, the Sopwith Salamander, which entered service in October 1918 but was too late to see combat. The Snipe was also fitted with the ABC Dragonfly, a powerful but temperamental radial engine, to produce the Sopwith Dragon, of which 200 airframes were built, but the failure of the Dragonfly power unit meant no Dragons would enter service either. The Snipe, meanwhile, despite proving inferior to the Martinsyde F.4 Buzzard in official tests, was selected to become the post-war RAF's standard single-seat fighter mainly because it was 25 per cent cheaper than the Buzzard and was not powered by a French engine. The Snipe, therefore, remained in frontline fighter service until 1926 and was used as a trainer until the following year.

Sopwith 7F.1 Snipe
Weight (Maximum take-off): 916kg (2020lb)
Dimensions: Length 6.05m (19ft 10in), Wingspan 9.47m (31ft 1in), Height 2.9m (9ft 6in)
Powerplant: one 170kW (230hp) Bentley BR2 nine-cylinder air-cooled rotary piston engine
Maximum speed: 195km/h (121mph)
Endurance: 3 hours
Ceiling: 5900m (19,500ft)
Crew: one
Armament: two 7.7mm (0.303in) Vickers machine guns fixed firing forward in fuselage decking

Sopwith Snipe
This aircraft was flown by Wiliam Barker during an engagement on 27 October 1918 in which he single-handedly fought a formation of 15 Fokker D.VIIs. E8102 features his personal red devil mascot on the Vickers machine gun and its fuselage is preserved today in Ottawa, Canada.

TWO-SEATER FIGHTERS & RECONNAISSANCE

At the start of the war, reconnaissance was considered by far the most important task that could be performed by aircraft, and it was the specific needs of this mission that dictated the design of the first truly mass-produced British aircraft, the B.E.2, but would ultimately render it terrifically vulnerable. Later British two-seaters were more belligerent, culminating in the outstanding Bristol F.2b.

This chapter includes the following aircraft:

- Royal Aircraft Factory B.E.2
- Vickers F.B.5 'Gunbus'
- Royal Aircraft Factory F.E.2
- Avro 504
- Caudron G.3
- Morane-Saulnier Type L and Type P
- Morane-Saulnier BB
- Royal Aircraft Factory R.E.5 and R.E.7
- Sopwith 1½ Strutter
- Royal Aircraft Factory R.E.8
- Armstrong Whitworth F.K.3
- Armstrong Whitworth F.K.8
- Bristol F.2 Fighter

A Sopwith 1¹/₂ Strutter biplane aircraft taking off from a platform built on top of the midships Q turret on HMAS *Australia*, an Indefatigable-class battlecruiser (1918).

TWO-SEATER FIGHTERS & RECONNAISSANCE

Royal Aircraft Factory B.E.2

By far the most important and numerous British aircraft for the first two years of the war, the ubiquitous B.E.2 proved highly vulnerable to German fighters and sparked political controversy.

B.E. stood for 'Bleriot Experimental' and referred to the tractor configuration of the aircraft, as opposed to pusher 'Farman' types, as the Bleriot was considered the archetypical tractor type in the early 1910s. Only a single example of the B.E.1 was built, chief designer Geoffrey de Havilland taking it up on its first flight in December 1911, powered by a 45kW (60hp) water-cooled Wolseley engine taken from a Voisin pusher aircraft. The B.E.1 was later re-engined with an air-cooled Renault engine of the same power and was engaged for several years on various test and research programmes until being struck off charge in mid-1916.

Immediate success

The B.E.2, however, initially differed only in its engine, the 45kW (60hp) Renault (later replaced by a 52kW (70hp) unit), and the fact that it had equal span wings. It flew for the first time in February 1912 and was destined to be produced in large quantities. The aircraft enjoyed early plaudits when it was flown extensively at the British Army's Military Aeroplane Competition on Salisbury Plain during August 1912, but as it was a government design, the B.E.2 was ineligible for the competition, hardly surprising when one considers that Mervyn O'Gorman, Director of the Royal Aircraft Factory, was one of the competition judges. Nonetheless, the B.E.2 demonstrated its obvious superiority to the other entrants, not least on 12 August 1912 when it achieved a British altitude record of 3220m (10,560ft), and the first order for the production B.E.2a was placed with arms giant Vickers shortly after. The first serial production aircraft appeared in early 1913, and two entered service with No.2 Squadron RFC in February. In pre-war use, the B.E.2 was noted for its high standard of serviceability and reliability as compared to contemporary aircraft and was followed by the B.E.2b, which was very similar to the earlier model but differed most obviously from its predecessor in that it introduced

RAF B.E.2b

A B.E.2b, built by Hewlett & Blondeau and delivered in October 1914, 705 was allocated to the Central Flying School and shows the very early RFC markings of Union Flags on the rudder and wings. These were soon dropped as they could be mistaken for the German Maltese cross markings from a distance.

decking between the two crew positions to form two distinct cockpits as opposed to the large dual cockpit of the B.E.2a.

On the outbreak of war in August 1914, both subtypes of B.E.2 made up part of the first three Army squadrons to fly to France with a B.E.2a of No.2 Squadron becoming the first RFC aircraft to arrive in France after the start of World War I.

B.E.2c ups and downs

Development had by this time shifted to the B.E.2c, a quite substantial redesign of the aircraft under the direction of engineer Edward Busk aimed to make the aircraft inherently

TWO-SEATER FIGHTERS & RECONNAISSANCE

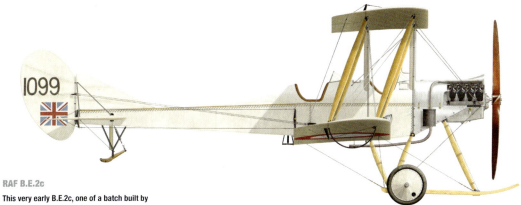

RAF B.E.2c
This very early B.E.2c, one of a batch built by Beardmore was operated by the RNAS at Whitley Bay during the autumn of 1915. Early naval wing roundels were red and white only as can be seen under the lower wings.

stable, this being seen as desirable both for safety reasons and for reconnaissance or observation duties as it allowed for better results with contemporary plate cameras that required a relatively long exposure time. This decision was to have grave consequences when it became clear that the inherent stability of the aircraft meant it could not manoeuvre quickly, leaving the B.E.2c terribly vulnerable to enemy fighter aircraft, but in the early months of 1914, the concept of aerial combat as it developed over the Western Front was more or less inconceivable and the fighter aircraft simply didn't exist. The B.E.2c first flew on 30 May 1914 and featured ailerons in place of wing-warping for lateral control, a pronounced forward stagger between the upper and lower wings and a new tailplane

Royal Aircraft Factory B.E.2c
Weight (Maximum take-off): 1066kg (2350lb)
Dimensions: Length 8.31m (27ft 3in), Wingspan 11.28m (37ft), Height 3.39m (11ft 2in)
Powerplant: one 67kW (90hp) RAF 1a V-8 air-cooled piston engine
Maximum speed: 116km/h (72mph)
Endurance: 3 hours 15 minutes
Ceiling: 3000m (10,000ft)
Crew: two
Armament: typically, one 7.7mm (0.303in) Lewis machine gun flexibly mounted between front and rear cockpits; up to 102kg (224lb) bomb load (when flown as a single seater)

RAF B.E.2c
A later production B.E.2c of No.12 Squadron RFC, 2502 was allocated to 'C' flight, hence the large letter on the cowling. This aircraft was shot down by Hans Immelman of Jasta 2 on 9 November 1916.

51

TWO-SEATER FIGHTERS & RECONNAISSANCE

RAF B.E.2c

Based at Hounslow in 1916 for nocturnal Home Defence duties, this B.E.2c is marked with the "white circle the same size as the blue circle used in the marking of day machines" as specified in the RFC's 12 September 1916 'Special Insignia for Night Flying Aircraft' notice.

Royal Aircraft Factory B.E.2c
Weight (Maximum take-off): 1066kg (2350lb)
Dimensions: Length 8.31m (27ft 3in), Wingspan 11.28m (37ft), Height 3.39m (11ft 2in)
Powerplant: one 67kW (90hp) RAF 1a V-8 air-cooled piston engine
Maximum speed: 116km/h (72mph)
Endurance: 3 hours 15 minutes
Ceiling: 3000m (10,000ft)
Crew: two
Armament: typically, one 7.7mm (0.303in) Lewis machine gun flexibly mounted between front and rear cockpits; up to 102kg (224lb) bomb load (when flown as a single seater)

---

with a triangular fixed vertical fin. Later production aircraft featured a fin of greater area to aid in spin recovery. Apart from the very first examples, B.E.2cs also featured the RAF 1A engine, which offered a modest improvement in power over the Renault used in earlier versions.

The first B.E.2cs were sent to France in small numbers in late 1914, but the first unit wholly equipped with the type, No. 8 Squadron RFC arrived in March 1915. Initial B.E.2c use was highly satisfactory, with aircraft used in the main for reconnaissance whilst making the occasional bombing attack, for example, the daring solo bombing mission on the airship sheds at Gontrode, made by Lieutenant Lanoe Hawker in late April 1915. The B.E.2c also undertook the RFC's first night raid on the night of 19/20 February when two B.E.2cs of No. 4 Squadron flown

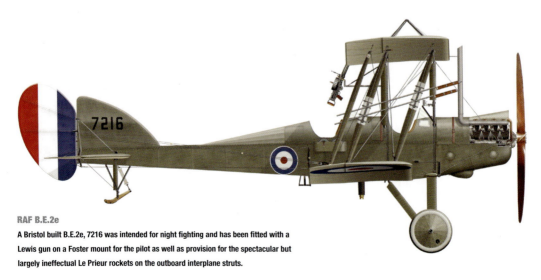

RAF B.E.2e

A Bristol built B.E.2e, 7216 was intended for night fighting and has been fitted with a Lewis gun on a Foster mount for the pilot as well as provision for the spectacular but largely ineffectual Le Prieur rockets on the outboard interplane struts.

TWO-SEATER FIGHTERS & RECONNAISSANCE

by Captains Horsfall and Tennant attacked Cambrai aerodrome, Tennant dropping his seven 9kg (20lb) bombs on the hangars from around 9m (30ft). Horsfall's two 50kg (112lb) bombs failed to release, however, though both eventually fell off as the aircraft returned to its aerodrome.

Cold meat

Although it proved dependable and delivered safe but unspectacular service, from late 1915, the B.E.2c became increasingly vulnerable to the attentions of a totally new kind of aircraft in the form of the Fokker E.I 'Eindecker', the world's first truly successful single-seat fighter. Unable to manoeuvre quickly nor outrun the Fokker monoplane, crews attempted to fit defensive armament to the aircraft but this was not easy.

The observer's cockpit ahead of the pilots was surrounded on all sides by wings and struts, a seating arrangement that had already compelled the pilot to operate the camera on reconnaissance missions as the lower wing was in the way if the observer attempted to take pictures. With the pilot seated behind the observer, fitment of a trainable machine gun to protect against attack from the rear was, at best, problematic and required the observer to fire over the pilot's head. Losses inexorably climbed as more Eindeckers appeared at the Front rising to a peak in early 1916, leading to the popular press terming B.E.2 crews as 'Fokker Fodder', whilst German fighter pilots chillingly referred to the B.E.2c as *kaltes fleisch* (cold meat).

Eventually, the situation was raised in Parliament when MP Noel Pemberton-Billing (founder of the Supermarine aircraft company) claimed B.E.2 crews were being "rather murdered than killed". As is often the case, the situation was more nuanced than it appeared, the B.E.2c subsequently enjoyed the *lowest* loss rate of any RFC type in the second half of 1916 due to improvements in tactics and the appearance of effective escort fighters, but the reputation of the aircraft never recovered.

Later development saw the appearance of the B.E.2d, a dual-control version that was mostly used as a trainer, though Belgium operated this type with a more powerful Hispano-Suiza engine and with the crew positions sensibly reversed. This was followed by the conventional B.E.2e, which introduced a new set

---

Royal Aircraft Factory B.E.2f
Weight (Maximum take-off): 1066kg (2350lb)
Dimensions: Length 8.31m (27ft 3in), Wingspan 11.28m (37ft), Height 3.39m (11ft 2in)
Powerplant: one 67kW (90hp) RAF 1a V-8 air-cooled piston engine
Maximum speed: 116km/h (72mph)
Endurance: 3 hours 15 minutes
Ceiling: 3000m (10,000ft)
Crew: two
Armament: two 7.7mm (0.303in) Lewis machine guns pointing forwards and rearwards; rack for 9kg (20lb) Cooper bombs

---

RAF B.E.2f
A B.E.2f (a hybrid variant consisting of a B.E.2c with B.E.2e wings) equipped with forward and rear pointing Lewis guns as well as a rack for 9kg (20lb) Cooper bombs, this No.10 Sqn RFC aircraft was lost during a night attack on the railhead at Hénin, near Douai in April 1917.

53

TWO-SEATER FIGHTERS & RECONNAISSANCE

RAF B.E.2c
This typically anonymous B.E.2c was built by the traction engine manufacturer Ruston Proctor in Lincoln. Its eventual fate was unknown, the aircraft was simply posted 'missing' on 27 April 1917.

of wings with a longer span upper plane, similar to that used on the R.E.8 as well as a new tail design. Developed in 1916, the expected higher power RAF 1b engine never entered production so the B.E.2e made do with the same RAF 1a as its predecessor and possessed a similar pedestrian performance.

Anti-Zeppelin role
Although the B.E.2 was, in the words of ace Albert Ball "a bloody awful aeroplane", it did prove relatively effective in one niche combat role as an anti-Zeppelin aircraft. Operated as a single seater with extra fuel and armed with an upward-angled Lewis gun firing a mixture of explosive and incendiary ammunition, the B.E.2c was the standard British Home Defence aircraft until the introduction of the Gotha bombers.

For this role, the aircraft's stability was a positive asset, for it simplified night flying and made the aircraft a steady gun platform. Five enemy airships were shot down by B.E.2c night fighters, including SL 11, the first to be brought down on British soil. Attempts to develop a day-flying fighter from the B.E.2 met with less success, however; as well as the B.E.12 single seater, the B.E.2c was modified into the frankly terrifying B.E.9 'pulpit' fighter in which, to overcome the absence of a reliable gun synchronizer, a small nacelle containing a gunner and machine gun were mounted directly *ahead* of the propeller. The single example built was sent to France for operational evaluation but was described by the Commander of 19 Squadron, Major Hugh Dowding, as "an extremely dangerous machine from the passenger's point of view",

and production did not ensue, its layout being rendered superfluous by the appearance of the reliable Constantinesco gun synchronizer gear, itself first fitted to a B.E.2c for testing in August 1916, that would transform British fighter design. Ultimately, approximately 3500 B.E.2s were built in total by around 20 contractors, though exact production figures are not known.

B.E.2a, Serial No. 347 pictured on a British airfield. In 1914, this was the first British aircraft to land in France following the outbreak of war.

54

TWO-SEATER FIGHTERS & RECONNAISSANCE

Vickers F.B.5 'Gunbus'

The Vickers F.B.5 was slow, unwieldy and quickly outclassed, but it was also incredibly significant, as this was the World's first operational purpose-built fighter aircraft.

Vickers had been developing the concept of an armed aircraft specifically designed to engage and destroy other aircraft from as early as 1912. The first such machine to actually be built was named the 'Destroyer', though it was later designated the E.F.B.1. Displayed at the Olympia Aero Show in 1913, it crashed on its first flight. Designer Archie Low persisted with the idea, however, and development culminated in the F.B.5 ('Fighting Biplane 5').

Making its maiden flight on 17 July 1914, less than a month before Britain declared war on Germany, the F.B.5 featured a pusher layout to allow a clear field of fire in the nose for a gunner armed with a single Lewis gun. The modest power of its Gnome Monosoupape rotary engine could propel it to the giddy heights of 110km/h (70mph) at 1500m (4920ft), an altitude it could achieve in 16 minutes: not particularly impressive figures even for 1914.

Initial delivery

The first of 207 F.B.5s was delivered to the RFC in November 1914 and the novelty of an aircraft possessing machine gun armament led to the enduring nickname of 'Gunbus' being conferred upon it. In service in France from February 1915, aircraft were initially allocated in ones and twos to squadrons operating other types until July 1915 when No. 11 Squadron RFC, wholly equipped with the type, deployed to Villers-Bretonneux in France to become the first operational fighter squadron in the World.

The first victory was achieved on 28 July by Welsh pilot Lionel Rees and gunner James McKinley Hargreaves, this only crew to achieve five victories

Vickers F.B.5

Weight (Maximum take-off): 930kg (2050lb)
Dimensions: Length 27ft 2in (8.28 m), Wingspan 36ft 6in (11.13m), Height 11ft 0in (3.35m) **Powerplant:** one 75kW (100hp) Gnome Monosoupape nine-cylinder air-cooled rotary piston engine
Maximum speed: 110km/h (70mph)
Endurance: 4 hours 30 minutes
Ceiling: 1500m (4920ft)
Crew: two
Armament: one 7.7mm (0.303in) Lewis machine gun flexibly mounted in nose

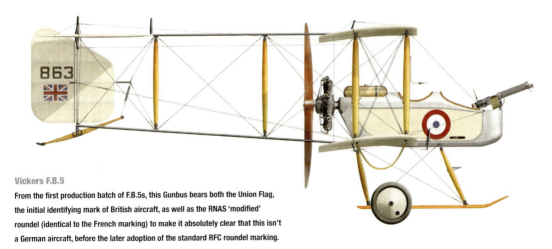

Vickers F.B.5
From the first production batch of F.B.5s, this Gunbus bears both the Union Flag, the initial identifying mark of British aircraft, as well as the RNAS 'modified' roundel (identical to the French marking) to make it absolutely clear that this isn't a German aircraft, before the later adoption of the standard RFC roundel marking.

TWO-SEATER FIGHTERS & RECONNAISSANCE

while flying the type to become the sole Gunbus 'aces'. The appearance of the Fokker Eindecker later in the year rendered the Gunbus effectively obsolete, and the introduction of more capable Allied single-seaters saw it gradually withdrawn from the front, though shortages in the supply of more modern two-seaters, such as the F.E.2b, would result in the F.B.5 and the slightly updated F.B.9 soldiering on in frontline service until July 1916, after which both types were used as trainers.

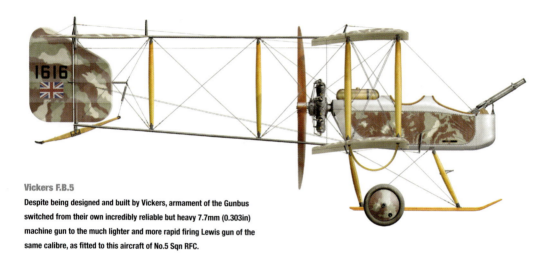

Vickers F.B.5
Despite being designed and built by Vickers, armament of the Gunbus switched from their own incredibly reliable but heavy 7.7mm (0.303in) machine gun to the much lighter and more rapid firing Lewis gun of the same calibre, as fitted to this aircraft of No.5 Sqn RFC.

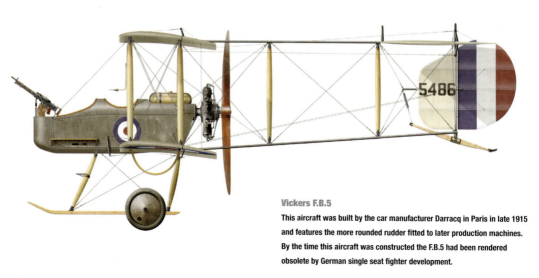

Vickers F.B.5
This aircraft was built by the car manufacturer Darracq in Paris in late 1915 and features the more rounded rudder fitted to later production machines. By the time this aircraft was constructed the F.B.5 had been rendered obsolete by German single seat fighter development.

TWO-SEATER FIGHTERS & RECONNAISSANCE

Royal Aircraft Factory F.E.2

Despite its anachronistic appearance, the F.E.2 series proved to be one of the most successful of the early war British aircraft designs, continuing to be operated as a night bomber long after its career as a two-seat fighter had ended.

RAF F.E.2b
Built by G & J Weir of Glasgow in 1916, this F.E.2b is pictured in the slightly unusual overall grey colour scheme it wore when serving with No. 11 Sqn RFC. Based at Izel-lès-Hameau in northern France it was crewed by second Lts E Burton and FW Griffiths.

Confusingly, but reflecting the absurdly incoherent designation systems typical of early British military aircraft, the designation F.E.2 (standing for Farman Experimental 2) was used for three completely separate aircraft designs linked only by their general layout. The first F.E.2 was designed and flown by Geoffrey de Havilland in 1911, and only one was built.

Curiously, de Havilland would work on the later iterations of the F.E.2 design and develop the D.H.1 for Airco after leaving the Royal Aircraft Factory, of which 100 were built and which was externally nearly identical to the definitive F.E.2a of 1914. The first F.E.2 was modified to carry a Maxim machine gun in the nose, but by 1913, a new F.E.2 had been built of greater strength and of distinctly more modern appearance. It featured the outer wings of the B.E.2a but crashed in early 1914.

A clear step up

The third F.E.2 design was of a different calibre entirely, intended as a fighter from the start; it was much stronger and more powerful and featured a flexibly mounted Lewis machine gun in the front cockpit able to cover an enormous field of fire. Featuring the outer wings of the B.E.2c, this new F.E.2 was initially powered by a six-cylinder 75kW (100hp) Green engine when it made its first flight in February 1914, but this was found to be underpowered, and it was replaced by an 89kW (120hp) Beardmore unit in production machines.

Only 12 of the initial F.E.2a variant were produced before production switched to the improved F.E.2b, initially fitted with the same 120hp Beardmore engine as the F.E.2a but later with a 119kW (160hp) unit. The newer variant deleted an airbrake that had been fitted to the F.E.2a but which

Royal Aircraft Factory F.E.2b

Weight (Maximum take-off): 1378kg (3037lb)
Dimensions: Length 9.83m (32ft 3in), Wingspan 14.55m (47ft 9in), Height 3.86m (12ft 8in)
Powerplant: one 120kW (160hp) Beardmore six-cylinder water-cooled piston engine
Maximum speed: 147km/h (92mph)
Endurance: 3 hours
Ceiling: 3400m (11,000ft)
Crew: two
Armament: two 7.7mm (0.303in) Lewis machine guns flexibly mounted at front and rear of front cockpit; up to 235kg (517lb) bombload

57

TWO-SEATER FIGHTERS & RECONNAISSANCE

RAF F.E.2b
On the strength of 22 Sqn RFC, 4883 was used by its improbably named Canadian commanding officer Major Chester Stairs Duffus to send an Albatros D.I 'out of control' on 16 October 1916. This was the third of his eventual five victories, all achieved whilst flying F.E.2bs.

had been found in practice to have little braking effect and added the provision to carry bombs or a camera, bestowing a true multi-role capability on The F.E.2b. Early F.E.2bs featured the same single machine gun armament as the F.E.2a but soon were being produced with a second Lewis gun, mounted on a telescopic mounting fitted between the front and rear cockpits and intended to be fired directly forward by the pilot over the observer/gunner's head. In practice, this second weapon was actually used by the gunner in the opposite direction as it could be fired backwards over the top wing to give a measure of protection to the rear, thus at least partly answering a common criticism of two-seater pusher types.

RFC service as the Fee
The F.E.2a was taken into service with No.6 Squadron RFC in May 1915, which operated the type in a mixed force, typical for the period, in conjunction with some B.E.2cs and a Bristol Scout. However, the first unit to be exclusively F.E.2 equipped was No. 20 Squadron RFC, which flew their F.E.2bs to France in January 1916. Initially, the F.E.2b enjoyed considerable success as a fighter and is credited, along with the Nieuport scouts and the D.H.2, with ending the period of supremacy enjoyed by German fighters known as the 'Fokker Scourge' due to the seeming

RAF F.E.2b
In overall black finish for its nocturnal role, A852 served with No. 100 Squadron RFC. This aircraft was lost and its crew captured after being hit by ground fire and a balloon cable whilst attacking Trier railway station, this being the longest ranged F.E.2b bombing mission ever attempted.

TWO-SEATER FIGHTERS & RECONNAISSANCE

invincibility of the Fokker Eindecker. Emblematic of this switch in fortune from Germans to Allies was the fact that on 18 June 1916, the first German air ace Max Immelman was killed in combat with F.E.2bs of 25 Squadron RFC, though it remains unknown if his Eindecker was shot down by the British aircraft or whether it suffered catastrophic structural failure. The 'Fee', as it became affectionately known, was largely popular with pilots due to its pleasant handling characteristics and its great structural strength. By contrast, the observer/gunner had a precarious position in the nose with no seatbelt, nor parachute, and only his grip on the cockpit sides or the gun to prevent him from falling out: a position made even more perilous if he were required to stand up and use the rearward facing gun as his entire body from the knees upward were exposed. To be fair to the F.E.2, however, this unenviable crew position was effectively inherent to two-seat pusher designs and was no different to that found in the Vickers F.B.5 or Farman M.F.11. A notable F.E.2b gunner was Captain Frederick Libby, the first American to become an 'ace',

who attained 10 victories as an F.E.2b gunner before scoring another four after becoming a pilot. In total, just under 50 F.E.2 crew members would achieve ace status with five or more victories.

Further variants

Further development of the aircraft resulted in the F.E.2c, an experimental variant that switched the crew positions to improve the pilot's view for nocturnal missions, but which did not enter production. The F.E.2d was the last production model and was largely similar to the F.E.2b but benefitted from the addition of a 186kW (250hp) Rolls-Royce Eagle engine, which improved performance at high altitude. The increased power also allowed for a heavier payload and allowed the F.E.2d to be fitted with a fixed, forward-firing machine gun for the pilot in addition to the existing pair of guns operated by the observer, thus making the F.E.2d one of the most heavily armed fighters then in service.

Three-hundred-and-eighty-six F.E.2ds were built, arriving at the front in the summer of 1916 and proving quite formidable, at least until the next

RAF F.E.2b

A presentation F.E.2b, A5448 was the second such machine paid for by public subscription by the citizens of New South Wales and named 'The White Edenglassie'. Built by Boulton & Paul of Norwich, it is depicted in factory fresh condition before allocation to a squadron.

Royal Aircraft Factory F.E.2b

Weight (Maximum take-off): 1378kg (3037lb)
Dimensions: Length 9.83m (32ft 3in), Wingspan 14.55m (47ft 9in), Height 3.86m (12ft 8in)
Powerplant: one 120kW (160hp) Beardmore six-cylinder water-cooled piston engine
Maximum speed: 147km/h (92mph)
Endurance: 3 hours
Ceiling: 3400m (11,000ft)
Crew: two
Armament: two 7.7mm (0.303in) Lewis machine guns flexibly mounted at front and rear of front cockpit; up to 235kg (517lb) bombload

59

TWO-SEATER FIGHTERS & RECONNAISSANCE

generation of German fighters began to be encountered towards the end of that year. The first victim of the Albatros D.I was an F.E.2b, and the aircraft's career as a fighter would be over by the autumn of 1917, in daylight hours at least. Even late in its fighting career, the F.E.2 could prove a tough opponent, however – in July 1917, Manfred von Richthofen suffered a serious head wound in combat with F.E.2ds, which kept him out of action for a month, from which, it is conjectured, he never fully recovered. In the same action, the crew of Captain D. C. Cunnell and Second Lieutenant A. E. Woodbridge, who were credited with injuring Richthofen, shot down four German fighters.

Night bombing success

By this time, the F.E.2 had already flown its first nocturnal bombing mission, and this would become the primary mission of the type, primarily as it proved comparatively easy to fly at night. Although the F.E.2d was replaced by the Bristol F.2b, the F.E.2b proved an unexpected success in the nocturnal light bombing role against a variety of targets as well as flying sorties that would later become known as 'intruder' missions to attack targets of opportunity. For the latter role, an F.E.2b with a highly modified nacelle carrying the crew side by side and fitted with a 37mm Vickers QF 1-pounder 'pom-pom' gun was developed. This proved effective when it worked but was unreliable and did not enter widespread service. Conventional F.E.2bs remained in service as night bombers until the Armistice, and the aircraft was so successful that although only 15 new F.E.2bs were built in the first quarter of 1918,

Engines
The pusher engine installation was popular amongst British crews as F.E.2d pilot Lt. W.C. Cambray explained: "we were told we would have Bristol Fighters to replace the F.E.2ds. We were not at all pleased, as the pusher's rear-mounted engine gave the Hun something to fire into and was a protection for the pilot and observer. The Bristol, being a tractor machine, made the observer feel he was a rather easy meal."

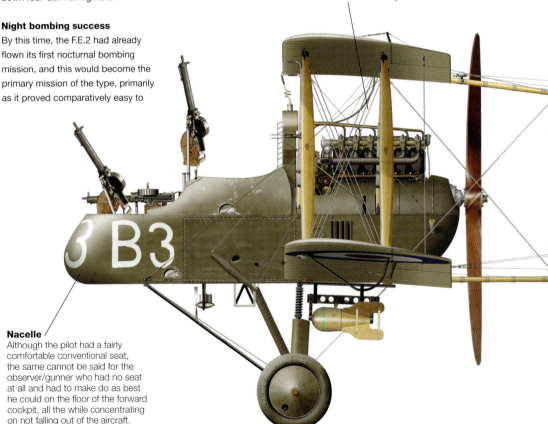

Nacelle
Although the pilot had a fairly comfortable conventional seat, the same cannot be said for the observer/gunner who had no seat at all and had to make do as best he could on the floor of the forward cockpit, all the while concentrating on not falling out of the aircraft.

TWO-SEATER FIGHTERS & RECONNAISSANCE

production subsequently increased, and a further 527 were built from April 1918 until the end of the war, at that point equipping six British and one American squadron. Typical missions included those undertaken during the Battle of Passchendaele when attacks were delivered against enemy aerodromes and railway junctions. For example, on the night of 16/17 August No. 102 Squadron RFC dropped a total of 4572kg (4½ tons) of bombs in attacks on Mouveaux aerodrome and railway stations at Menin, Courtrai, Comines and Roulers. Both the F.E.2b and F.E.2d also saw service with night-fighting Home Defence squadrons for Zeppelin interception duties, but neither possessed sufficient altitude performance to prove effective in this role; on at least two occasions, Zeppelins were sighted but could not be engaged by attacking F.E.2s simply because they could not climb to the airship's altitude.

After November 1918, the F.E.2 quickly disappeared from the RAF inventory, but the F.E.2d was modified by Vickers into a training aircraft with a new dual control nacelle to become the 'Vickers Instructional machine'. All 35 converted aircraft were supplied to China, with deliveries beginning in 1920.

Royal Aircraft Factory F.E.2d

Weight (Maximum take-off): 1378kg (3037lb)
Dimensions: Length 9.83m (32ft 3in), Wingspan 14.6m (47ft 9in), Height 3.9m (12ft 8in)
Powerplant: one 186kW (250hp) Rolls-Royce Eagle liquid cooled V-12 piston engine
Maximum speed: 156km/h (97mph)
Endurance: 3 hours 30 minutes
Ceiling: 5181m (17,000ft)
Crew: two
Armament: one (sometimes two) 7.7mm (0.303in) Lewis machine guns fixed, firing forward in nacelle, two 7.7mm (0.303in) Lewis machine guns flexibly mounted at front and rear of front cockpit; up to 68kg (150lb) bombload

Tail booms
The pusher layout was used for many British designs, such that British troops were instructed to fire on anything that had a propeller in the nose (which was unfortunate for B.E.2 crews). Apparently German fighter pilots referred to such types as 'lattice tails'.

RAF F.E.2d
An F.E.2d of No.57 Squadron RFC, A6355 was patrolling near Noyelles on the morning of 29 April 1917 when it was shot down by Unteroffizier F. Gille of Jasta 12. Its crew of Second Lts E. Percival and F.A.W. Handley were taken prisoner.

TWO-SEATER FIGHTERS & RECONNAISSANCE

Avro 504

The most-produced British biplane and fifth-most-produced British aircraft of all time, the Avro 504 enjoyed a successful combat career in the early years of the war before becoming a ubiquitous training aircraft used for decades to train thousands of pilots.

Avro 504A

Somewhat alarming to modern eyes, this swastika bedecked Avro 504A was serving as a trainer with No. 65 Sqn at Sedgeford in Norfolk in late 1917. The swastika at this time had no political connotations and was merely a good luck symbol widely used on both sides of the conflict.

In 1909, Alliot Verdon Roe built the first British aircraft powered by a British engine to fly, and by 1912, his first truly successful aircraft, the Avro 500, entered limited production, with a total of 18 being built. The Avro 504, however, which was derived from the 500, would be built in numbers totalling over 11,000, making it the most produced aircraft of any nation to have served in World War I. The immense success of the 504 is all the more staggering when one considers its modest performance, barely able to exceed 150km/h (93mph), though its pleasant flying characteristics and docile handling made it ideal as a training aircraft and the majority of production aircraft were built for this purpose. In the initial stages of the war, however, the 504 was widely employed in combat and achieved several aviation firsts.

Early fame and production

Flying for the first time in September 1913, powered by a 60kW (80hp) Gnome Lambda, the initial 504 as built featured unusual warping ailerons for lateral control, though these were quickly discarded in favour of conventional hinged ailerons. The first 504 led a busy life operating both on wheels and floats, it flew in competitions, was used to promote the Daily Mail newspaper, and set an unofficial British altitude record at 4570m (15,000ft). At the outbreak of war, this aircraft was requisitioned for military use but was written off when the engine failed as it was making its delivery flight to its new owners. By

Avro 504A

Weight (Maximum take-off): 771kg (1700lb)
Dimensions: Length 8.97m (29ft 5in), Wingspan 10.97m (36ft), Height 3.18m (10ft 5in)
Powerplant: one 60kW (80hp) Le Rhône, or 60kW (80hp) Gnome 9-cylinder air-cooled rotary piston engine
Maximum speed: 138km/h (86mph)
Endurance: 4 hours 30 minutes
Ceiling: 3960m, 13,000ft
Crew: one or two
Armament: usually none but 36kg (80lb) bombload fitted on underfuselage racks for Zeppelin shed raid

TWO-SEATER FIGHTERS & RECONNAISSANCE

Avro 504A
Another Avro 504A, A491 was serving in 1915 with an unknown unit whilst sporting this somewhat unusual colour scheme and thistle motif on the fuselage. The 504A was the first 504 variant to be built in large numbers.

this time, however, production Avro 504s were already in service use – an order for 12 had been placed by the War Office in the early summer of 1914 while the Admiralty ordered a solitary example. A few of the RFC Avros had been delivered in time to be flown to France at the outbreak of hostilities, but initial service use demonstrated the aircraft had an inadequate range, leading to an increase in fuel capacity allowing for a 4 ½ hour endurance. As was typical in the very early days of military flying, the Avro 504s were issued piecemeal to units operating a selection of aircraft types, and no frontline squadron was ever wholly equipped with the type.

Strafing attack
During 1914, Avro 504s became the first British aircraft to engage in ground attack by strafing troops, but a 504 was also the first British aircraft to be shot down when an aircraft of No. 5 Squadron RFC was downed by ground fire on 22 August. Revenge of a sort came three days later when observer Lieutenant Euan Rabagliati managed to use a rifle to bring down a German Taube monoplane from an Avro 504 flown by Second Lieutenant C. W. Wilson, thus scoring the first British air-to-air victory. The Avro 504 also undertook one of the first strategic bombing raids in history when, on 21 November, three examples set off from France and flew over Lake Constance to attack the Zeppelin works at

Avro 504AJ
The fuselage marking belies the Australian ownership of this otherwise anonymous Avro 504J. The J and K models were essentially identical but the 504K could be fitted with a wider array of engines.

TWO-SEATER FIGHTERS & RECONNAISSANCE

Friedrichshafen, managing to destroy the hydrogen-generating plant and scoring hits on the airship sheds.

Transition to training

The aircraft soon became obsolete as a frontline machine and settled into its role as a near-ubiquitous training aircraft. The principal variants were the Avro 504J, which was powered by a 75kW (100hp) Gnome, and the 504K, which had 'universal' engine bearers able to accept a variety of engines based on availability. These two variants were the first to be built in truly enormous quantities, and 8340 504s were built by the time of the Armistice.

Despite its switch to the training role, the 504 did see further use as a combat aircraft beginning in late 1917 when there was a serious need for an aircraft with better performance than the B.E.2c to act as night fighters. Accordingly, 274 Avro 504J and 504Ks were converted into single-seaters, armed with a Lewis gun above the wing on a Foster mounting, and issued to eight Home Defence fighter squadrons. Surprisingly, 226 of these aircraft were still fully operational in this role at the end of the war. Following the end of hostilities, the Avro 504J was declared obsolete in 1921, but the 504K would serve the RAF for many years to come, gradually being replaced by the Avro 504N, a post-war version with an Armstrong-Siddeley Lynx radial engine, of which 592 were built between 1925 and 1932, though the 504 began to be replaced by the Avro Tutor in 1933.

The next largest user of the 504 was the Soviet Union, which operated a few British-built examples as well as building a copy designated the U-1 in large numbers. Popular amongst Soviet pilots, the 504 and its U-1 clone were collectively referred to by the diminutive *Avrushka* (or 'Little Avro') and served widely until replaced by the Polikarpov Po-2.

Avro 504K

In service with No. 33 squadron during 1918, E3259 was an Avro 504K employed as a Home Defence night fighter. The forward cockpit has been faired over, white elements have been removed from the markings to reduce their nocturnal visibility and a Lewis gun is fitted above the top wing.

Avro 504K

Weight (Maximum take-off): 830kg (1829lb)
Dimensions: Length 8.97m (29ft 5in), Wingspan 10.97m (36ft), Height 3.18m (10ft 5in)
Powerplant: one 82kW (110hp) Le Rhône 9J nine-cylinder air-cooled rotary piston engine
Maximum speed: 153km/h (95mph)
Range: 400km (250 miles)
Ceiling: 4900m (16,000ft)
Crew: two
Armament: optional 7.7mm (0.303in) Lewis machine gun fixed firing forward above top wing

TWO-SEATER FIGHTERS & RECONNAISSANCE

Caudron G.3

Widely used in the early stages of World War I, the G.3 proved successful until the advent of single-seat fighters, coupled with its ponderous performance, rendered it prohibitively vulnerable for frontline use.

The Caudron brothers developed a distinctive twin-boom layout biplane with a small fuselage pod in the years immediately prior to the outbreak of war, and the G.3 conformed to this tested but somewhat unusual layout. Developed from the slightly smaller G.2, of which ten were built, the G.3 was specifically intended for military use and made its maiden flight in May 1914. Following the outbreak of war, as one of the best of the varied crop of early military aircraft available to the Allies, the G.3 was in great demand, and an impressive total of 2849 were built, around half by other companies, both in Italy and the UK as well as France, the Caudron brothers having patriotically waived their right to a licence fee.

Caudron G.3
(N)3066 was utilised by the RNAS Flying School at Vendome aerodrome in 1917. A Caudron G.3 that survived the war to be entered onto the Belgian civil register is currently displayed in the RAF Museum at Hendon, UK, in these markings.

Suited to reconnaissance
Although occasionally used as a bombing aircraft, the G.3 was primarily used for reconnaissance and proved ideal for the role, being both stable and easy to fly. In service with Escadrille C.11 of the French *Aéronautique Militaire* on the outbreak of war, the Caudron was immediately plunged into action and initially proved effective. Most G.3s were of the A2 model for artillery spotting and widely employed on the Western Front, in Russia and the Middle East. Eventually, the lack of defensive armament, limited manoeuvrability, and pedestrian performance of the G.3 would see the aircraft removed from operations over the Western Front in mid-1916, though it persisted for a time in less demanding theatres, the RFC continuing to use theirs until October 1917 by which time it was totally obsolete.

The D2 and E2 versions were trainer variants, the main function of the Caudron after mid-1916, and the aircraft persisted in this role until as late as 1931 in China. An unusual training variant of the G.3 was the R1 (for *Rouler* or 'Roller'), with cut-down wings to train pilots in taxiing, one of very few aircraft types specifically designed to be unable to fly.

Caudron G.3
Weight (Maximum take-off): 710kg (1565lb)
Dimensions: Length 6.4 m (21ft 0in), Wingspan 13.4m (44ft 0in), Height 2.5m (8ft 2in)
Powerplant: one 60kW (80hp) Le Rhône 9C 9-cylinder air-cooled rotary piston engine
Maximum speed: 106km/h (66 mph)
Endurance: 4 hours
Ceiling: 4300m (14,100ft)
Crew: two
Armament: usually none

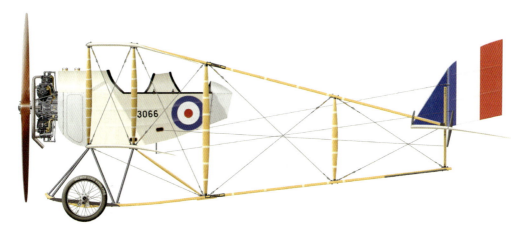

65

TWO-SEATER FIGHTERS & RECONNAISSANCE

Morane-Saulnier Type L and Type P

Morane Saulnier's parasol monoplanes were amongst the most successful of early war French aircraft and were used by virtually all the Allied powers. The Type L was responsible for two notable 'firsts' in aerial warfare.

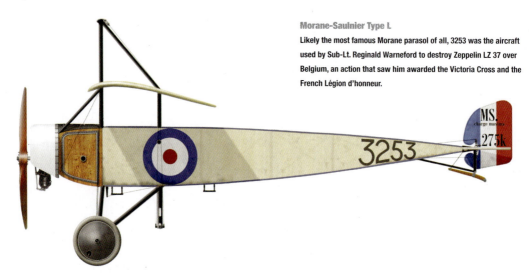

Morane-Saulnier Type L
Likely the most famous Morane parasol of all, 3253 was the aircraft used by Sub-Lt. Reginald Warneford to destroy Zeppelin LZ 37 over Belgium, an action that saw him awarded the Victoria Cross and the French Légion d'honneur.

First flown in August 1913, the Type L was utilized as both a single and twin-seat aircraft and used, like most of its contemporaries, as a jack of all trades, turning its hand to reconnaissance, light bombing, and artillery observation as the need arose. However, in early 1915, the Type L made history by becoming the first true Allied single-seat fighter aircraft when French pilot Raymond Garros fitted wedge-shaped deflector plates to the propeller blades of his Type L, allowing a machine gun to fire directly ahead, and shot down three German aircraft during April before being captured at the end of the month.

Another first
During the same year, Type Ls started to be used by British units, 50 examples were delivered to the RFC and a further 25 went to the RNAS. It was one of the latter, flown as a single seater, that achieved the first air-to-air 'kill' of a Zeppelin when on 7 June 1915, one of these aircraft, flown by Flight Sub-Lieutenant Reginald Warneford of 1 Squadron RNAS intercepted the Zeppelin LZ 37 and destroyed it by dropping six 9kg (20lb) bombs on it, a feat for which he was awarded the Victoria Cross.

Type LA and Type P
The Type L was further developed into the Type LA with slightly better streamlining, and then the Type P, a strengthened and aerodynamically improved aircraft that was produced in three major variants based on which engine was fitted. One of these, the MS.24, featured the same 60kW (80hp) Le Rhône as the earlier Type LA and was produced exclusively for RFC use, supplementing earlier Moranes in RFC units, although examples of both other variants were also taken on strength by British units.

Morane Saulnier Type L
Weight (Maximum take-off): 667.5kg (1472lb)
Dimensions: Length 6.88m (22ft 7in), Wingspan 11.2m (36ft 9in), Height 3.93m (12ft 11in)
Powerplant: one 60kW (80hp) Le Rhône 9C 9-cylinder air-cooled rotary piston engine
Maximum speed: 125km/h (78mph)
Endurance: 4 hours
Ceiling: 3658m (12,000ft)
Crew: one or two
Armament: one optional 7.7mm (0.303in) Lewis machine gun fixed forward firing on nose cowling

TWO-SEATER FIGHTERS & RECONNAISSANCE

Morane-Saulnier BB

Built to a British order, the Morane Saulnier BB was destined never to serve with its native France, all production machines being supplied to the United Kingdom and Russia.

A departure from the prevailing norm for the Morane-Saulnier company, every previous aircraft they had produced was a monoplane and the BB was their first biplane design. Consisting of the fuselage and tail surfaces of the earlier Type P monoplane fitted with a conventional set of biplane wings, 16 were supplied to Russia, but the remaining 94 production aircraft were supplied to the United Kingdom. The BB also served to illustrate the inadequacy of British aircraft production during the first two years of war, unable to produce sufficient aircraft for their own needs, British forces had to procure aircraft from France.

Seating setup and limited numbers

The BB was intended to be powered by the 110hp Le Rhône 9J, which delivered a fairly high top speed compared to other two-seaters, but shortages of this engine meant most BBs had to make do with the 80hp Le Rhône 9C. Unlike many contemporary two-seat aircraft, the BB adopted the definitive seating arrangement of pilot in the front seat and observer at the rear, with the latter crew member being provided with a flexibly mounted Lewis gun for defence. Despite the relatively small numbers produced, the BB would ultimately equip four RFC squadrons and a further three RNAS units, though it was only well into 1916 that squadrons began to be equipped with a single aircraft type, and the BB had been in service since the previous year. By the end of 1916, however, the aircraft was essentially obsolete and was withdrawn from the front line. In service, the BB's relatively good performance saw it employed also as a two-seat fighter, with a second Lewis gun mounted on the top wing, firing forward over the propeller arc.

Morane-Saulnier Type BB
Weight (Maximum take-off): 750kg (1650lb)
Dimensions: Length 7m (23ft), Wingspan 8.65m (28ft 5in), Height 2.54m (8ft 4in)
Powerplant: one 82kW (110hp) Le Rhône 9Ja nine-cylinder air-cooled rotary piston engine
Maximum speed: 147km/h (92mph)
Endurance: 2 hours
Ceiling: 4000m (13,000ft)
Crew: one or two
Armament: one 7.7mm (0.303in) Lewis machine gun flexibly mounted in rear cockpit; one optional 7.7mm (0.303in) Lewis machine gun fixed forward firing above wing

Morane-Saulnier BB
The first of its type to enter RNAS service, 3683 was assigned to No. 4 Sqn RNAS. two machine guns were usually carried, both operated by the observer, though the aircraft was also flown as a single seater with the overwing gun fired by the pilot.

TWO-SEATER FIGHTERS & RECONNAISSANCE

Royal Aircraft Factory R.E.5 and R.E.7

The R.E.5 and its R.E.7 development were typical of the general-purpose two-seaters produced in the lead-up to and first year of war. Dependable but slow and lacking in manoeuvrability, they proved unable to defend themselves against single-seat fighters.

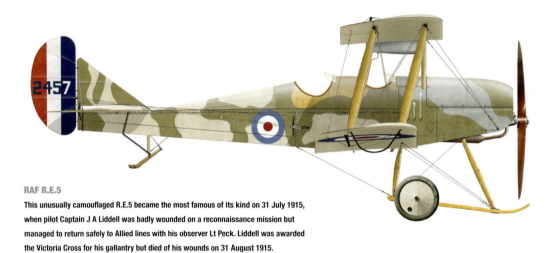

RAF R.E.5
This unusually camouflaged R.E.5 became the most famous of its kind on 31 July 1915, when pilot Captain J A Liddell was badly wounded on a reconnaissance mission but managed to return safely to Allied lines with his observer Lt Peck. Liddell was awarded the Victoria Cross for his gallantry but died of his wounds on 31 August 1915.

Seeking to produce a superior aircraft to the successful B.E.2, single examples of the R.E.1, R.E.2, and R.E.3 (R.E. standing for 'Reconnaissance Experimental') were built before the outbreak of war, testing different wing designs and engines. The R.E.4 was intended to have better landing characteristics, but there is no evidence that it was actually built. The R.E.5 that followed, however, did enter production, although only 24 were built, 11 of which saw action in France. A pre-war design, the R.E.5 utilized an 89kW (120hp) Austro-Daimler engine, making it more powerful than the B.E.2 and featuring wings of greater span. Extended wings of greater span still were fitted to a few R.E.5s for high-altitude research flights, and one of these aircraft gained brief fame by achieving the official absolute height record of 5760m (18,900ft) on 14 May 1914.

R.E.7 adaptation and usage
The R.E.5 was further developed into the R.E.7, a slightly larger and more powerful aircraft intended to perform the same reconnaissance and bombing missions as its predecessor but also expected to undertake escort missions. For obvious reasons, the Austrian-built Austro-Daimler engine was no longer available for British use by 1915, so a switch was made to the 112kW (150hp) RAF 4a, and the aircraft utilized a modified set of the extended span wings developed for the R.E.5. Of the 230 R.E.7s produced, around a quarter served in France following the type's operational debut in early 1916. Sadly, the R.E.7 did not prove very popular, as by mid 1916, its slow speed and low ceiling when carrying a bomb load rendered it very vulnerable to attack, and the outdated cockpit arrangement of pilot at the rear and observer/gunner in front was ill-suited for combat, though at least two R.E.7s were converted to a three-seat configuration, with a new position added for a gunner behind the pilot. Most R.E.7s, however, served as trainers and target tugs.

Royal Aircraft Factory R.E.7
Weight (Maximum take-off): 1565kg (3450lb)
Dimensions: Length 9.72m (31ft 11in), Wingspan 17.37m (57ft), Height 3.84m (12ft 7in)
Powerplant: one 112kW (150hp) RAF 4a V-12 air-cooled piston engine
Maximum speed: 135km/h (84mph)
Endurance: six hours
Ceiling: 1980m (6500ft)
Crew: two
Armament: one 7.7mm (0.303in) Lewis machine gun flexibly mounted in front cockpit; up to 147kg (324lb) bombload

TWO-SEATER FIGHTERS & RECONNAISSANCE

Sopwith 1½ Strutter

The strangely named 1½ Strutter was the only Sopwith two-seater to see service during the war. Despite seeing widespread service with both the RFC and RNAS, by far the largest user was, surprisingly, France.

Sopwith 1½ Strutter

The strangely named 1½ Strutter was the only Sopwith two-seater to see service during the war. Despite being heavily used by both the RFC and RNAS, by far the largest operator was, surprisingly, France.

Sopwith 1½ Strutter

Weight (Maximum take-off): 977kg (2154lb)
Dimensions: Length 7.7m (25ft 3in), Wingspan 10.21m (33ft 6in), Height 3.12m (10ft 3in)
Powerplant: one 97kW (130hp) Clerget 9B 9-cylinder air-cooled rotary piston engine
Maximum speed: 160km/h (100mph)
Endurance: 3 hours 45 minutes
Ceiling: 4700m (15,500ft)
Crew: two
Armament: one 7.7mm (0.303in) Vickers machine gun fixed firing forward on nose cowling and one 7.7mm (0.303in) Lewis gun flexibly mounted in rear cockpit; up to 60kg (130lb) bombload

Sopwith had developed a two-seater in late 1914 that was in appearance very much like an enlarged Sopwith Tabloid. The pressure of work at the Kingston factory meant the new aircraft, known as 'Sigrid's Bus' after the Works Manager Fred Sigrist, took a considerable time to complete but set a new British altitude record on the same day as its maiden flight on 5 June 1915.

LCT design

This aircraft formed the basis for a larger two-seat fighter, initially referred to as the LCT (for 'Land Clerget Tractor') and designed by Herbert Smith. The LCT featured an unusual strut arrangement of one short and one long strut supporting the top wing arranged at four points around the front cockpit, forming a 'W' shape when viewed from directly in front, and this is believed to be the origin of the 1½ Strutter nickname, though officially the aircraft was the Type 9700 in the RNAS and simply the Sopwith Two-Seater in the RFC. Flown for the first time in December 1915, the aircraft boasted the then unusual features of a variable incidence tailplane and twin airbrakes on either side of the fuselage and, significantly, was fitted with a synchronized Vickers machine gun for the pilot, the first Allied aircraft to be so equipped, though shortages in synchronizer gear meant some early production aircraft featured only the rear gun. The Scarff ring for the observer's trainable Lewis gun in the rear cockpit was also new, and deliveries of this piece of equipment were initially slow enough to delay 1½ Strutter production at times.

Mid-war production

Production deliveries of the 1½ Strutter began to be received at the RNAS in February 1916, and the first unit to

69

TWO-SEATER FIGHTERS & RECONNAISSANCE

equip with the aircraft was one flight of No. 5 Wing RNAS. The Sopwiths were used to escort the wing's Caudron G.4 bombers, as well as being used as bombing aircraft themselves, and the type also flew anti-submarine patrols in the Mediterranean. Some RNAS machines were delivered as dedicated bombers with no rear cockpit, the weight saved allowing for a greater bombload. The RFC also placed an order for 1½ Strutters, but Sopwith was overburdened with supplying the Admiralty's needs, and the Army's aircraft were built by subcontractors Vickers and Ruston Proctor.

Battle of the Somme

Desperately requiring aircraft in the lead-up to the Battle of the Somme, the RNAS agreed to allow the transfer of enough aircraft to allow for No. 70 Squadron RFC to equip on the type in the summer of 1916. Initial operations with the type proved successful, the 1½ Strutter was pleasant to fly, well-armed and long ranged and could mount offensive patrols deep into enemy territory. Unfortunately, newer German fighters, such as the potent Albatros fighters with much greater performance, started to enter widespread service in early 1917, and the 1½ Strutter was effectively outclassed. Like other contemporary Sopwith designs, it was quite lightly constructed and could not take much punishment, it was too stable to make a good dogfighter and communication between the pilot and the observer was impeded by the large gap between the front and rear cockpits.

Gradually withdrawn from the front, the last operational 1½ Strutters in the RFC were replaced by Sopwith Camels in late October 1917. The type served on in Home Defence units, and some were altered to a single seater layout for use against Zeppelins, with the pilot seated in the rear cockpit and an armament changed to one or two Lewis guns, on Foster mounts or fixed to fire forwards and upwards. In this form, they were known as the Sopwith Comic.

RNAS's use of the 1½ Strutter concentrated on shipborne use, the aircraft's excellent handling and lightweight making it ideal for these operations. Known as the 'Ship's Strutter', the aircraft served on the early aircraft carriers HMS *Furious* and *Vindex* as well as operating from platforms fitted to the gun turrets of some larger capital ships such as HMS *Repulse*.

Extensive French usage

By far the largest user and producer of the 1½ Strutter, however, was France In the absence of a suitable

---

Sopwith 1½ Strutter

Weight (Maximum take-off): 977kg (2154lb)
Dimensions: Length 7.7m (25ft 3in), Wingspan 10.21m (33ft 6in), Height 3.12m (10ft 3in)
Powerplant: one 97kW (130hp) Clerget 9B 9-cylinder air-cooled rotary piston engine
Maximum speed: 160km/h (100mph)
Endurance: 3 hours 45 minutes
Ceiling: 4700m (15,500ft)
Crew: two
Armament: one 7.7mm (0.303in) Vickers machine gun fixed firing forward on nose cowling and one 7.7mm (0.303in) Lewis gun flexibly mounted in rear cockpit; up to 60kg (130lb) bombload

---

Sopwith 1½ Strutter
A8226 was used by C Flight of No.45 Squadron during 1917. Whilst being flown by Captain L.W. MacArthur with observer 2nd Lt A.S. Carey, the aircraft was shot down by Leutnant Max von Muller of Jagdstaffel 28 to become his thirteenth of an eventual 38 combat victories.

TWO-SEATER FIGHTERS & RECONNAISSANCE

Sopwith 1½ Strutter
The 1½ Strutters of 3 Wing RNAS featured colourful individual aircraft markings behind the fuselage roundel such as the red circle in a white square sported by 9730 in the winter of 1916/17. This aircraft was flown on occasion by future high scoring Canadian ace Raymond Collishaw.

replacement for obsolescent pusher Breguet and Farman bombers, the *Aviation Militaire* had been forced to look abroad for an alternative design and settled on the promising Sopwith. Produced in three versions, the SOP. 1A.2 (two-seat reconnaissance), SOP. 1B.2 (two-seat bomber) and SOP. 1B.1 (single-seat bomber), approximately 4500 1½ Strutters were built in France, compared to 1429 in the UK. French use of the Sopwith design was widespread with many bomber and artillery-observation squadrons operating the type, though the introduction of the aircraft to French units was somewhat delayed and it was already outclassed by German fighters by the time it reached the front. French aircrew also complained that their licence-built Sopwiths were inferior to British-built machines, and although appreciated for its handling, the type was widely regarded as an underwhelming combat aircraft.

Post combat use
Delays in the introduction of the superior Breguet 14 and Salmson 2 saw the French forced to soldier on with the type, and over half of the Army Corps reconnaissance squadrons were still equipped with it in early 1918. Like the RFC and RNAS, after its withdrawal from combat, the French utilized the 1½ Strutter as a trainer due to its excellent flying qualities and continued to use the type in this role well into the 1920s. Three Belgian squadrons also flew Sopwith two-seaters during the conflict, operating a mix of British and French-built machines, and many other nations flew the type post-war.

The end of the war did not spell the end of service for the Strutter. One of many air arms to operate the two-seat Sopwith postwar was the US Navy which, like the RNAS before it, utilised the Strutter to develop operations from flying-off platforms mounted on battleship gun turrets. This overall grey Sopwith, with hydrovane mounted ahead of the undercarriage, was photographed being hoisted aboard USS *Oklahoma* in Guantanamo Bay, Cuba, circa 1921.

TWO-SEATER FIGHTERS & RECONNAISSANCE

Royal Aircraft Factory R.E.8

More difficult to fly than the forgiving B.E.2, the R.E.8 gained an unfortunate reputation in early service, and though this improved, the R.E.8 was never a popular aircraft despite being produced in large numbers.

During 1915, it became clear that the B.E.2c was obsolescent, and the RFC headquarters in France drew up a statement of requirements for a new two-seater based on operational experience, particularly emphasizing the need for any new aircraft of this type to be able to defend itself. The Royal Aircraft Factory responded with a totally new design that bore no relationship to the previous members of the R.E. series – the R.E.8.

Beset by problems

Designed by John Kenworthy and Walter Barling, the R.E.8 first flew on 17 June 1916. The most obvious change from its predecessors was the cockpit arrangement with the gunner now seated at the rear, allowing for a much greater field of fire and, crucially, placing the machine gun in the ideal position to defend against attacks from the rear and above, the most natural approach for an attacking single-seater. The pilot was also provided with a synchronized Vickers gun firing directly forwards, fitted to the port side of the fuselage. Unusually, the rear fuselage was angled upwards towards the empennage, giving the aircraft a very distinctive tail-up stance in flight. This design was to allow the wing incidence to be angled upwards when on landing, causing the large wing surfaces to provide a braking effect and allow the aircraft to use short fields

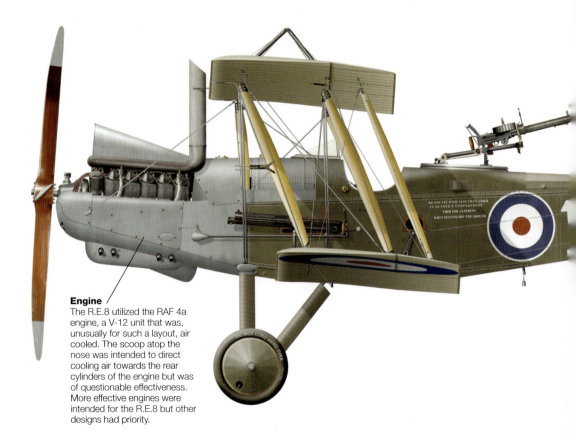

Engine
The R.E.8 utilized the RAF 4a engine, a V-12 unit that was, unusually for such a layout, air cooled. The scoop atop the nose was intended to direct cooling air towards the rear cylinders of the engine but was of questionable effectiveness. More effective engines were intended for the R.E.8 but other designs had priority.

TWO-SEATER FIGHTERS & RECONNAISSANCE

with safety. Unfortunately, this was problematic for inexperienced pilots, as in the three-point flying attitude, the nose seemed absurdly high, an effect compounded by the shape and position of the engine's large air scoop directly in front of the pilot. Many pilots failed to appreciate the need for bringing the stick well back on landing and overshot the landing area as a result.

This was far from the R.E.8's only troublesome design feature, however, as the aircraft had been designed, like the B.E. series before it, with inherent in-flight stability, in the mistaken belief that this was a particularly desirable characteristic for an observation aircraft. As a direct result, the R.E.8 was not very manoeuvrable. Compounding this particular problem was the unusually small tail fin and rudder, the size of both being smaller on production machines than the prototype, which was believed to be the culprit for a worryingly large number of fatal crashes caused by stalls and spins when the aircraft entered active service with No. 52 Squadron in France during November 1916. So severe were the losses that the R.E.8 was withdrawn and 52 Squadron re-equipped on the B.E.2e, which it had been flying beforehand, which did nothing for the aircraft's reputation.

Despite this, the conversion of other squadrons to the R.E.8 proceeded at a high pace, and the accident rate fell somewhat, as aircrew became accustomed to the peculiarities of their new equipment.

Unfortunately, the R.E.8 proved to be a distinctly inadequate combat aircraft. For example, on 13 April 1917, six R.E.8s of No. 59 Squadron set off on a reconnaissance mission, two carrying cameras and the remainder acting as escorts. Intercepted by six German fighters, all the R.E.8s were shot down within minutes, and ten aircrew were killed. Nonetheless, despite, rather than because of, any inherent qualities of the aircraft, things did improve for the R.E.8 units, and the aircraft ultimately delivered adequate, if unspectacular, service in its intended functions of light bombing, reconnaissance and artillery spotting, both during the day and by night.

One obvious design change saw an increase in the area of the vertical tail surfaces, which improved handling and largely eradicated the stall and

Controls
Unusually for an aircraft of its era, attempts were made to ease the R.E.8 pilot's workload. The tailplane incidence could be adjusted in flight and an early form of rudder trim (applied to the rudder bar) was fitted to alleviate the constant pressure required to counteract the torque generated by the propeller.

RAF R.E.8
Weight (Maximum take-off): 1301kg (2869lb)
Dimensions: Length 8.5m (27ft 11in), Wingspan 12.98m (42ft 7in), Height 3.47m (11ft 5in)
Powerplant: one 100kW (140hp) Royal Aircraft Factory RAF 4a V-12 air-cooled piston engine,
Maximum speed: 166km/h (103mph)
Endurance: 4 hours 15 minutes
Ceiling: 4100m (13,500ft)
Crew: two
Armament: one 7.7mm (0.303in) fixed forward-firing Vickers gun on port side of forward fuselage, and one or two 7.7mm (0.303in) Lewis guns flexibly mounted in rear cockpit; up to 102kg (224lb) bombload

RAF R.E.8
Based at Droglandt aerodrome in the north of France during 1917, A3224 was an early production R.E.8 serving with No. 21 Squadron and wears its distinctive dumbbell unit marking on the fuselage sides.

TWO-SEATER FIGHTERS & RECONNAISSANCE

RAF R.E.8

Many contractors built the R.E.8 as the Royal Aircraft Factory had relatively limited manufacturing capacity. C5048 was constructed by the Coventry Ordnance Works in November 1917 and issued to No.16 Sqn RFC.

RAF R.E.8

Sporting the enlarged dorsal and ventral fin at the tail and the deeper engine sump typical of later production R.E.8s, B5106 was on the strength of No. 59 Squadron RAF, at Vert-Galland Aerodrome, near Rouen during May 1918.

spin issues. Very late production aircraft eventually received an even larger, curved fin, which improved handling yet further, and for the first time visually appeared to be in proportion to the rest of the airframe. A few R.E.8 crews also proved that the aircraft *could* successfully be flown aggressively, and despite being designed as a bomber, one crew became aces on the type; the pairing of Lieutenants Croye Pithey and Hervey Rhodes of No. 12 Squadron were credited with ten air-to-air victories whilst flying the R.E.8. A measure of the aircraft's eventual acceptance can be gleaned from its affectionate rhyming slang nickname of 'Harry Tate', after a highly popular music hall comedian.

Nonetheless, the aircraft was always regarded as inferior to its contemporary, the Armstrong Whitworth F.K.8 and plans to replace the R.E.8 with a Sunbeam Arab-powered variant of the superlative Bristol F.2 came to naught due to insufficient availability of the Sunbeam engine before the war's end.

In total, 4077 examples of the R.E.8 were eventually built, with contracts for a further 353 cancelled following the armistice. As well as British and Commonwealth squadrons, a single Belgian squadron operated the type, eventually re-engining their R.E.8s with the 149kW (200hp) Hispano-Suiza in a distinctive circular cowling.

Following the end of the war, the R.E.8 was quickly withdrawn from service, and perhaps unsurprisingly, not a single example was registered for civilian use.

TWO-SEATER FIGHTERS & RECONNAISSANCE

Armstrong Whitworth F.K.3

Although not adopted for service over the Western Front, the F.K.3 was used operationally in the Balkans. The 'Little Ack' also proved to be an invaluable training machine and was built in large numbers.

Designed by the Dutch designer Frederick Koolhoven, hence the 'F.K.' designation, the F.K.3 was intended as an improved version of the B.E.2c, which Armstrong Whitworth was building under government contract. Designed in early 1915, the F.K.3 flew for the first time in August and externally appeared little changed from its B.E. progenitor. Under the skin, however, the aircraft featured a much-simplified structure that was considerably easier to build, which did away with welded joints and complex metal parts. The upper wing was given greater dihedral, and although the first seven production machines featured the same Renault engine and seating arrangement as earlier the B.E.2, with observer in front and pilot behind, the remainder of the approximately 500 production aircraft featured a more powerful RAF 1A engine, a new fin and rudder design, and reversed the positions of the crew.

Limited frontline use

Although the F.K.3 possessed a slightly improved performance over the B.E.2, the increase was not deemed sufficient to warrant taking the aircraft into service with operational squadrons in France, especially with the considerably more capable F.K.8 and R.E.8 already in development. Frontline use of the F.K.3 was therefore limited to No. 47 Squadron RFC which flew the aircraft from Salonika on bombing and reconnaissance duties.

Curiously, one of 47 Squadron's F.K.3s landed in Bulgarian territory due to damage incurred in combat and was pressed into Bulgarian service. Reportedly popular with Bulgarian crews, this singular F.K.3 continued in service into 1918 and ultimately performed 42 nocturnal bombing missions against its former owners before being abandoned by its Bulgarian crew in British territory after being hit by ground fire.

Armstrong Whitworth F.K.3

B9554 was a late example of the 350 built by Hewlett & Blondeau, an aircraft manufacturer based in Luton. By the time it was manufactured, virtually all F.K.3s were serving with home-based training squadrons.

Armstrong Whitworth F.K.3
Weight (Maximum take-off): 933kg (2056lb)
Dimensions: Length 8.84m (29ft), Wingspan 12.21m (40ft), Height m (11ft 10in)
Powerplant: one 67kW (90hp) RAF 1A air-cooled V-8 piston engine
Maximum speed: 140km/h (87mph)
Endurance: 3 hours
Ceiling: 3700m (12,000ft)
Crew: two
Armament: one 7.7mm (0.303in) Lewis Gun flexibly mounted in rear cockpit; up to 51kg (112lb) bomb load (if flown as single seater)

TWO-SEATER FIGHTERS & RECONNAISSANCE

Armstrong Whitworth F.K.8

Although it possessed a distinctly pedestrian performance, the sturdy F.K.8 was a popular aircraft, held in higher regard than its rival, the R.E.8. Despite its excellent service record and large production run, the F.K.8 faded into obscurity after 1918.

Designed by Frederick Koolhoven as a replacement for the B.E.2 and Armstrong Whitworth's own F.K.3, the F.K.8 was larger, more powerful and much stronger than the earlier aircraft. First taking to the air in May 1916, a month before the appearance of the first R.E.8, an initial batch of fifty were ordered in case the Royal Aircraft Factory design should prove unsuccessful. Early experience with the R.E.8 would bear out the prudence of this approach, though ultimately several thousand more of this type would be built than the much more popular Armstrong Whitworth.

A profoundly conventional machine in most respects, the F.K.8 in its

Armstrong Whitworth F.K.8

Delivered to No. 35 Sqn RFC in November 1916, A2702 was damaged in a crash within a month but was repaired and back in service by February 1917. Subsequently issued to No.2 Aircraft Depot, whose markings it wears here, as well as the name 'Queenie II', A2702 was back with 35 Sqn by late August 1917.

TWO-SEATER FIGHTERS & RECONNAISSANCE

initial production guise featured a particularly angular engine cowling, an overcomplicated and cumbersome undercarriage, and tall twin radiators in an inverted vee over the forward fuselage, all of which combined to give the new aircraft a clumsy appearance. On operations, the undercarriage proved insufficiently strong to bear up to the rough nature of front-line aerodromes and the radiator design was susceptible to blockages. Both these issues were rectified relatively simply, at unit level the undercarriage was replaced by simpler Bristol F.2 undercarriage units from early 1917, though ultimately this led to a shortage in the Bristol units and the practice had to be stopped. After May 1918 however, F.K.8s were fitted with revised undercarriage from the factory. Radiator blockages were dealt with initially with improved tubes, but the unwieldy 'tower' type radiators were replaced with a much neater 'box' design fitted to the fuselage sides in later production machines. Later aircraft also benefited from a revised forward cowling of improved aerodynamic form and featured long exhaust pipes fitted

Armstrong Whitworth F.K.8
Weight (Maximum take-off): 1275kg (2811lb)
Dimensions: Length 9.58m (31ft 5in), Wingspan 13.26m (43ft 6in), Height 3.33m (10ft 11in)
Powerplant: one 119kW (160hp) Beardmore water-cooled six-cylinder inline engine
Maximum speed: 153km/h (95mph)
Endurance: 3 hours
Ceiling: 4000m (13,000ft)
Crew: two
Armament: one 7.7mm (0.303in) Vickers machine gun fixed, forward-firing in nose and one 7.7mm (0.303in) Lewis gun in the rear cockpit; up to 118kg (260lb) bomb load

Production changes
Although the cowling, undercarriage and radiator changes were obvious, the tail unit changed too, albeit subtly. Initial F.K.8s featured a rudder with a long pointed horn balance. This subsequently gave way to this design with a much blunter horn balance, more in keeping with the pugilistic overall aesthetic of the aircraft.

Unit markings
RFC, and after April 1918, RAF unit markings consisted of shapes and symbols painted on the fuselage rather than numbers or letters. The large white triangle on this F.K.3 denotes No.35 Squadron RFC. Sometimes these markings survived the conflict, the hexagon of 85 Squadron for example was applied to its Bristol Bloodhound Surface to Air missiles as late as 1991.

77

TWO-SEATER FIGHTERS & RECONNAISSANCE

to the fuselage sides in the manner of the Bristol Fighter. From the start, the F.K.8 featured the definitive crew arrangement of observer/gunner at the rear and pilot in front as well as a trainable Lewis gun in the rear cockpit the aircraft was fitted with a single Vickers gun firing forward. Initially fitted with Armstrong Whitworth's own mechanical synchronizer, this was replaced in later aircraft by the much more reliable Constantinescu hydraulic synchronization gear. Despite its use of a more powerful engine than that fitted to the R.E.8, the F.K.8 proved even slower, barely able to exceed 150km/h (93mph), despite this the aircraft was to prove effective in service and gave a good account of itself in aerial combat.

Big Ack and Little Ack

Entering active service in January 1917 with No. 35 Squadron in France, the F.K.8 would eventually equip six squadrons on the Western Front as well as a further three in the United Kingdom for Home Defence and another three in Palestine and Macedonia. Thanks to its docile handling, the F.K.8 was also widely employed as a training aircraft. On operations, the type proved very popular with crews thanks to its dependability, easy flying characteristics, and great strength, and garnered the nickname 'Big Ack' from its crews ('Ack' being the letter 'A' in the contemporary British Army phonetic alphabet) leading to the earlier F.K.3 being retrospectively named 'Little Ack'. Indicative of the toughness of the 'Big Ack' was the action fought by 18-year-old Second Lieutenant Alan A. McLeod and his observer, Lieutenant A. W. Hammond of No. 2 Squadron on 27 March 1918. Returning from a raid, they were attacked by a Fokker Dr.I, which Hammond promptly shot down, but seven more Fokkers appeared. McLeod shot down a second aircraft. Hammond downed two more, but both crew were heavily wounded, and the F.K.8 was hit so badly that the floor of the rear cockpit fell out.

Eventually, the fuel tank was hit, and flames engulfed the front cockpit. Incredibly, McLeod climbed out of the cockpit and onto the port wing, still under attack from the remaining Dr.Is, and managed to control the aircraft with one hand on the burning control column, side-slipping to keep the flames blowing broadly away from him until crash-landing in No-Man's-Land. McLeod dragged the unconscious Hammond from the F.K.8 and towards British troops, who rescued both airmen. McLeod would be awarded the Victoria Cross, one of two won by F.K.8 pilots, and Hammond lost a leg but was awarded a Bar to his Military Cross.

Post-war service

The F.K.8 remained in service until the armistice; like the R.E.8 it was intended to be replaced by a variant of the Bristol F.2 but issues with the Sunbeam engine prevented this from happening. F.K.8s did not remain in service for long following the end of hostilities, the last being withdrawn in Greece during September 1919, though a single example flew bombing and reconnaissance missions against rebel positions during the Paraguayan revolution of 1922. In addition, eight F.K.8s were civil registered in Australia, one of which conducted the first passenger-carrying service of the Queensland and Northern Territory Aerial Services, later to become QANTAS.

Armstrong Whitworth F.K.8
Although later aircraft benefitted from a less angular cowling, smaller 'box' radiators and a neater undercarriage design, it would be difficult to describe the F.K.8 as an aesthetically pleasing aircraft. This example was serving with No. 10 Sqn RAF at Abele, Belgium in October 1918.

TWO-SEATER FIGHTERS & RECONNAISSANCE

Bristol F.2

An outstanding aircraft, the Bristol fighter became the definitive British two-seater, serving with distinction over the Western Front. Its excellent performance and dependability saw it remain in frontline RAF service until 1932.

Bristol F.2B
Pictured with the distinctive scheme it wore when operating with No.1 Squadron Australian Flying Corps in Palestine during 1918, A7194 had previously served with No. 111 Squadron RFC during which time it had shot down at least five enemy aircraft.

Originally designed by Frank Barnwell to answer a requirement for an aircraft to replace the venerable B.E.2 series, a requirement that would lead to the production of the R.E.8 and F.K.8, the Bristol two-seater was intended to be powered by either an 89kW (120hp) Beardmore or a 112kW (150hp) Hispano-Suiza engine. However, the appearance of the Rolls-Royce Falcon, rated at 142kW (190hp), before construction of the original aircraft had commenced caused Barnwell to revise his design, and performance estimates with the Falcon were sufficiently impressive to suggest that the aircraft should instead be a fighter to replace the 1½ Strutter and F.E. series.

Design changes

The aircraft was constructed over the summer of 1916 to make its first flight on 9 September, initially fitted with a pair of B.E.2d wings as a timesaving measure, Bristol being major contractors for the type. Various major changes were made to the cowling to improve visibility, and the prominent endplate fins originally fitted to the lower wing were deleted, but the aircraft was found to be generally satisfactory and entered production as the Bristol F.2A. A notable feature of the new aircraft was the placing of the fuselage, roughly halfway between the upper and lower wings. This unusual positioning was chosen to put the upper wing directly in line with the pilot's line of sight and thus minimize its effect on visibility whilst avoiding the use of an overly deep fuselage.

The first F.2As were delivered just before Christmas 1916, and No. 48 Squadron RFC was the initial unit to convert to the type, flying to France in March 1917, but the aircraft was

Bristol F.2B
Weight (Maximum take-off): 1,471kg (3243lb)
Dimensions: Length 7.87m (25ft 10in), Wingspan 11.96m (39ft 3in), Height 2.97m (9ft 9in)
Powerplant: one 205kW (275hp) Rolls-Royce Falcon III V-12 liquid-cooled piston engine
Maximum speed: 198km/h (123mph)
Range: 594km (370 miles)
Ceiling: 5500m (18,000ft)
Crew: two
Armament: one 7.7mm (0.303in) Vickers machine gun 7.7mm) fixed firing forward in the fuselage nose and one or two 7.7mm (0.303in) Lewis machine guns flexibly mounted in rear cockpit; up to 110kg (240lb) bomb load

TWO-SEATER FIGHTERS & RECONNAISSANCE

Bristol F.2B
Eleven-victory ace Lt Sydney Oades used this aircraft to shoot down an Albatros D.V whilst serving with 139 Sqn RFC in Italy during January 1918. As noted in the fuselage inscription, A7300 was one of several aircraft acquired with funds supplied by Maharaja Rameshwar Singh of Darbhanga in the Mithila region of India and Nepal.

initially held back from combat. Trenchard wanted to wait until the opening of the Second Battle of Arras for the F.2A to make its combat debut and surprise the Germans with a new type.

The F.2A's debut certainly turned out to be surprising but absolutely not in the manner the RFC had intended: No.48's first patrol into enemy territory was met by five Albatros D.IIIs from the elite Jasta 11 led by the 'Red Baron', Manfred von Richthofen, and four of the six aircraft were shot down with a fifth badly damaged. This disastrous initial experience, however, was simply due to inexperience, crews accustomed to lower-performance two-seaters of weaker construction flew the F.2A in rigid formation in an attempt to maximize the crossfire of their rear gunners.

Configuration game changer
The Bristol fighter was, however, a strong, powerful, and manoeuvrable aircraft, and pilots soon realized that the aircraft could and should be flown like a single-seater, using the synchronized machine gun in the nose as the primary weapon, with the added benefit of a gunner to protect the rear. Once this lesson had been learned, the Bristol F.2 became the preeminent

Bristol F.2B
With the white of the roundels and tail stripes toned down for its role as a night fighter, it is believed that C4636 may have had the blue of its markings replaced by light grey. This aircraft was used by Lt. AJ Arkell and Air Mechanic ATC Stagg to shoot down a Gotha bomber over East London in May 1918.

TWO-SEATER FIGHTERS & RECONNAISSANCE

Bristol F.2B

Supplied to New Zealand as part of the Imperial Gift of 1919, H1557 was written off in a fatal training crash in 1926. Pilot Captain Frederick Horrell and a passenger Lewis Reid were killed but the trainee pilot survived, though with serious injuries.

two-seater of the war, and the combat capability of the aircraft was further enhanced by the appearance of the definitive F.2B, with the more powerful Falcon III engine resulting in a 24km/h (10mph) increase in speed and much better climb rate. Only 52 F.2As were ever built and the F.2B started to be received by squadrons in France as early as May of 1917, rapidly supplanting the earlier model in frontline units. Extremely popular with its crews, many of whom attained ace status, the F.2B gained the affectionate nicknames of 'Brisfit' and 'Biff'. The most successful F.2B pilot of all was Canadian Major Andrew McKeever, who achieved 31 victories against German aircraft and who flew with seven different rear gunners at various points in his career, several of whom became aces in their own right. Chief amongst them was Lieutenant Leslie Powell, who was, coincidentally, from Bristol, who attained 18 of his total of 19 aerial victories as McKeever's gunner. The highest-scoring gunner of all, however, was Lieutenant Charles Gass, who was credited with a remarkable total of 39 victories, all whilst flying in an F.2B, the highest score attained by any British or Commonwealth gunner during the conflict. Gass was flying with the Canadian pilot Lieutenant Alfred Atkey on 7 May 1918 when they shot down five enemy aircraft in a single day, managing to repeat the feat with five more shot down in a day just two days later. Atkey ended the war as a high scoring two-seater ace with 38 victories in total, 29 scored with the F.2b, the rest in the D.H.4.

Armament limitations

The Bristol Fighter's excellent flying qualities were not entirely matched by its firepower, one forward-firing Vickers gun was considered inadequate by late 1917, and as a result, although the single forward-firing gun remained the standard armament throughout the aircraft's production life, many aircraft were modified in the field to fit a Lewis gun on a Foster mount above the top wing. This mounting was offset to starboard to prevent it from interfering with the aircraft's compass, which was itself mounted on the trailing edge of the top wing in the pilot's direct line of sight. At least one aircraft was modified with two Lewis guns mounted on the top wing, though the weight and drag penalty of such an installation must have been considerable. The trainable Scarff ring mounting for the rear gunner's weapon also allowed for two Lewis guns to be fitted but this made the armament overly heavy to handle and aim, especially at higher altitudes, and many observer gunners preferred a single weapon. In general, however, the F.2B was proving more than satisfactory and plans were under way to equip all British two-seater squadrons with it, replacing the less combat-capable R.E.8 and F.K.8 in reconnaissance units. Sadly for the crews compelled to fly in these inferior aircraft, Rolls-Royce was unable to produce enough Falcon engines to meet demand, and delays were incurred whilst another engine was sought.

Attention fell upon the 200hp Sunbeam Arab, it being decided that Sunbeam-powered aircraft would be built by subcontractors and be supplied for reconnaissance and general-purpose use, while Bristol would continue to manufacture aircraft with the more powerful Rolls-Royce engine for fighter units. Unfortunately,

TWO-SEATER FIGHTERS & RECONNAISSANCE

the Sunbeam Arab suffered from serious developmental problems, and only a handful reached France before the Armistice and both the R.E.8 and F.K.8 soldiered on until the end of the conflict.

aircraft and the F.2B Mk.II was flown in 1919, which was specifically adapted for this role, equipped with desert equipment and a tropical cooling system. Four hundred and fifty-three of this variant would be built, followed by the Mk.III and Mk.IV, which differed little externally but featured structural improvements. Five thousand three hundred and twenty-nine F.2Bs were built in total, and 39 squadrons would be equipped with Bristol Fighters at

Busy post-war record
After hostilities ended, Bristol continued to manufacture the aircraft as well as refurbish existing airframes and upgrade aircraft for specific tasks and theatres. The Bristol Fighter was adopted as the RAF's standard army cooperation

Visibility
The unusual fuselage placement, carried on struts roughly halfway between the wings, was selected primarily to give the crew the maximum possible view for a conventional tractor biplane. Visibility in the upper hemisphere in particular was outstanding.

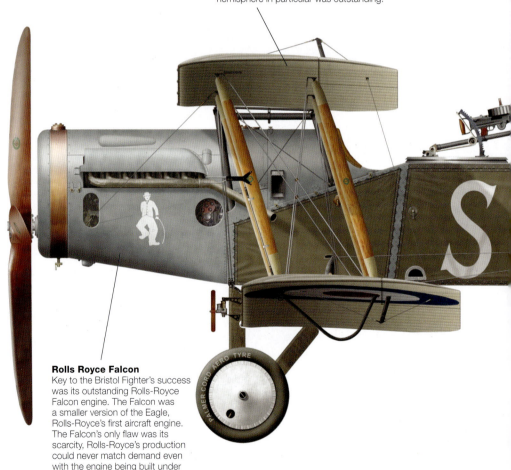

Rolls Royce Falcon
Key to the Bristol Fighter's success was its outstanding Rolls-Royce Falcon engine. The Falcon was a smaller version of the Eagle, Rolls-Royce's first aircraft engine. The Falcon's only flaw was its scarcity, Rolls-Royce's production could never match demand even with the engine being built under licence by Brazil-Straker in Bristol.

TWO-SEATER FIGHTERS & RECONNAISSANCE

some point in their existence. The very last Bristol F2Bs on RAF charge were operated until 1932 with No. 20 Squadron in India. The F.2B also found ready acceptance on the export market being combat-proven and relatively cheap due to the vast number of surplus aircraft that became readily available after November 1918.

The largest user of the aircraft after the RAF was Poland, which operated 106 F.2Bs, all but two of which were powered by Hispano-Suiza engines, and around 40 of these would see service during the Polish–Soviet War, participating in the decisive Battle of Warsaw. Like their British counterparts, Polish Bristol Fighters would serve until 1932. Belgium also adopted the type and built it under licence at SABCA. However, plans for large-scale production in the US (the aircraft had been personally championed by General Pershing, American Commander in Chief in France) floundered after it was decided to re-engine the aircraft with the Liberty L-12, which, though powerful, was too large and heavy for the airframe, rendering it problematically nose-heavy. Despite this issue, 2000 F.2Bs were ordered from Curtiss, designated the O-1, though only 27 were ultimately built. An American redesign featuring a new

Bristol F.2B
Weight (Maximum take-off): 1,471kg (3243lb)
Dimensions: Length 7.87m (25ft 10in), Wingspan 11.96m (39ft 3in), Height 2.97m (9ft 9in)
Powerplant: one 205kW (275hp) Rolls-Royce Falcon III V-12 liquid-cooled piston engine
Maximum speed: 198km/h (123mph)
Range: 594km (370 miles)
Ceiling: 5500m (18,000ft)
Crew: two
Armament: one 7.7mm (0.303in) Vickers machine gun 7.7mm) fixed firing forward in the fuselage nose and one or two 7.7mm (0.303in) Lewis machine guns flexibly mounted in rear cockpit; up to 110kg (240lb) bomb load

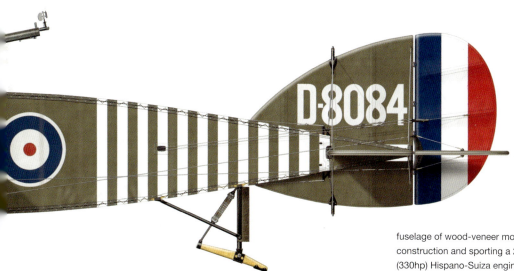

Bristol F.2B
As well as bearing the silhouette of Charlie Chaplin on the nose, this 139 Squadron aircraft features no fewer than 12 fuselage stripes (most squadron aircraft were painted with just two). During the summer of 1918, Captain Sydney Dalrymple and 2nd Lt Baldwin claimed at least four victories in this aircraft.

fuselage of wood-veneer monocoque construction and sporting a 246kW (330hp) Hispano-Suiza engine also entered limited production designated the XB-1A or XB-1B depending on the machine guns fitted, Marlin or Browning respectively. After three prototypes were constructed, 44 production XB-1s were built by the Dayton-Wright Company, but despite the extra power of the Hispano Suiza engine, their performance differed little from the original F.2B.

BOMBERS

Although the Army fielded the outstanding tactical bomber of the war in the shape of the D.H.4, it was the Royal Navy that was the driving force in the development of the strategic bomber. The Handley Page O/400 was the first true British 'heavy' and began the process that would ultimately lead to the same company's Halifax and the Avro Lancaster that spearheaded the colossal Bomber Command raids of the mid-1940s.

This chapter includes the following aircraft:

- Farman MF.11
- Voisin III
- Short Bomber
- Martinsyde Elephant
- Airco DH.4
- Airco DH.9 and DH.9A
- Sopwith T.1 Cuckoo
- Blackburn Kangaroo
- Vickers Vimy
- Caudron G.4
- Handley Page Type O

A ground crewman hands the observer of this Airco DH.4 a magazine of photographic plates before take off. Although designed as a bomber, the DH.4 was regularly used as a reconnaissance machine, a task at which it excelled, its high speed rendering it very difficult to intercept.

BOMBERS

Farman MF.11

Despite its fragile appearance, the MF.11 made history when an RNAS example conducted the first nocturnal bombing attack on the Western Front in December 1914.

Derived from the earlier MF.7, itself used quite extensively for reconnaissance in the first year of the war, the Maurice Farman MF.11 dispensed with the forward-mounted elevator of the earlier machine to become a conventional twin-boom pusher biplane.

Longhorn and Shorthorn

This difference between the two aircraft led to their British nicknames of 'Longhorn' in the case of the MF.7, with its prominent 'horns' ahead of the wings and cockpit to which the elevator was attached, and 'Shorthorn' for the MF.11 which had no 'horns' at all with the elevator fitted at the tail as had become effectively ubiquitous by the time of its first flight in 1913. Initially, the MF.11 featured the pilot's seat placed ahead of the observer in the nose of the fuselage nacelle, but operational experience combined with the increasing necessity of mounting a trainable machine gun in the nose of the aircraft saw the crew positions swapped, in this form the aircraft was sometimes referred to as the MF.11bis.

Of relatively large size, the Farman proved useful and saw extensive service with many nations during the first two years of the war, notably France, the UK, Russia, and Italy, who also produced it under licence. By the autumn of 1915, however, the Farman had become too vulnerable to enemy fighters, after which it enjoyed widespread success as a training aircraft.

A new era

Employed mostly as a reconnaissance machine during 1914 and 15, the MF.11 ushered in a new era in aerial warfare when, on the night of 21 December 1914, a single RNAS-operated aircraft attacked German gun emplacements near Ostend, the first night-bombing mission undertaken by a heavier-than-air aircraft. The type was also responsible for another first

As well as the regular MF.11 'Shorthorn' landplane, Farman also produced the MF.11 'Hydro' floatplane, a handful of which were acquired by the RNAS. This example, serial number 115 was pictured taxiing to shore just before the outbreak of hostilities in 1914.

Farman MF.11
Weight (Maximum take-off): 928kg (2046lb)
Dimensions: Length 9.45m (31ft), Wingspan 16.15m (53ft), Height 3.18m (10ft 5in)
Powerplant: one 75kW (101hp) Renault 8D V-8 air-cooled piston engine
Maximum speed: 106km/h (66mph)
Endurance: 3 hours 45 minutes
Ceiling: 3800m (12,500ft)
Crew: two
Armament: one 7.7mm (0.303in) Lewis gun machine gun flexibly mounted in nose, up to 131.5kg (288lb) bombload

when a Japanese example bombed the German cruiser SMS *Kaiserin Elisabeth*, becoming the first aircraft to attack an enemy ship, albeit unsuccessfully.

Voisin III

One of the most successful of the early war aircraft, the Voisin III was built under licence in Russia, Italy and the United Kingdom. Despite being used primarily as a bomber, the Voisin became the first armed aircraft in history to shoot down another in aerial combat with an installed machine gun.

The Voisin III was a re-engined version of the earlier Voisin L of 1912 and benefitted from the same steel-tube construction pioneered on the earlier aircraft, making it an unusually robust machine for the time. Appearing in early 1914, the Voisin III was one of the types on which the French decided to standardize in the lead up to war, and around 1350 were built in two similar variants, the LA and the LAS with a raised engine thrust line, making it one of the most numerous of early war aircraft. Many of these were the result of licence production with the Voisin built in Russia, Italy, and the UK, as well as France.

Multiple roles

Like most two-seat aircraft of its era, the Voisin was used for a variety of tasks, including reconnaissance, artillery spotting, and training. It was, however, for bombing, both by day and night, that the Voisin became best known, proving better suited to this role than contemporary Caudron and Farman machines, and Voisins formed the equipment of the world's first dedicated bombing squadrons. However, it was as a fighter (of sorts) that the Voisin III cemented its place in military aviation history: on 5 October 1914 Sergeant Joseph Frantz and Corporal Louis Quénault of Escadrille V.24 shot down a German Aviatik B. I flown by Oberleutnant Fritz von Zangen and Sergeant Wilhelm Schlichting near Reims, the first time an aircraft had brought down another using machine gun fire.

Both the RFC and RNAS utilized the Voisin LA, the former service being supplied with many aircraft supplied directly from France and the RNAS receiving 50 British-built examples. These were heavily employed on bombing and patrol missions, moving their sphere of operations to secondary theatres after the aircraft's very low speed and lack of manoeuvrability made its survival over the Western Front increasingly unlikely.

Voisin LA

Weight (Maximum take-off): 1350kg (2976lb)
Dimensions: Length 9.5m (31ft 2in), Wingspan 14.74m (48ft 4in), Height 2.95m (9ft 8in)
Powerplant: one 97kW (130hp) Salmson M.9 9-cylinder water-cooled radial piston engine
Maximum speed: 105km/h (65mph)
Range: 200km (120 miles)
Ceiling: 3500m (11,500ft)
Crew: two
Armament: one 7.7mm (0.303in) Lewis gun machine gun flexibly mounted in nose; up to 91kg (200lb) of bombs

Voisin III

This Voisin LA of the RNAS, 8501 was one of three such aircraft serving with 2 Wing and stationed on Imbros, a large Aegean island, during the Dardanelles campaign in 1915. All three Voisins were finished in this immaculate white scheme.

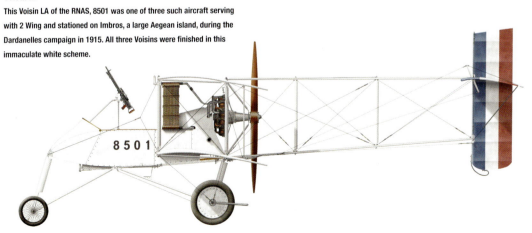

BOMBERS

Short Bomber

The first British purpose-designed bombing aircraft, the Short Bomber, was developed from successful Short seaplane designs. Underpowered and slow, though possessed of a great range, the Bomber's service life was short.

The Royal Navy took the lead in the development of British long-range strategic bombing aircraft, and it is therefore unsurprising therefore that the Admiralty should select Short Brothers, a significant producer of RNAS aircraft to design it.

Features and modifications

Essentially comprising a Short 184 seaplane fuselage fitted with wheeled undercarriage and a modified Short 166 wing of increased span, the Short Bomber was found in early testing to be unable to carry the required bombload, so the wingspan was increased by a further 3.66m (12ft). This modification was successful as far as payload was concerned but rendered the aircraft dangerously unstable, requiring an increase in fuselage length of 1.35m (4ft 5in) to cure the problem.

These modifications resulted in an unusually large single-engine aircraft, with a wingspan greater than most twin-engined bombers. They also seriously delayed the Bomber's service entry.

Service history

In service, the Short Bomber was welcomed for its impressive payload, as it was able to carry around four times more bombs than the Caudron G.4 (depending on fuel load). Range capability was also excellent, with the aircraft demonstrating a maximum endurance of six hours. Less impressive was the underpowered aircraft's speed performance, and by the time the delayed Bomber had entered service with No. 7 Squadron RNAS, the much superior Handley Page O/100 had already flown. As a result, the operational life of the Short Bomber, which had always been regarded as an interim type anyway, was notably brief.

The Bomber flew its first mission, a raid on Ostend, on 15 November 1916 and after a fairly intense period of operations over the winter of 1916 and 1917, flew its final series of raids, against Zeebrugge Mole, on four successive nights in April 1917.

Eighty-three Short Bombers were built in total, most of which served with the RNAS, though 15 were passed to the RFC to help make up for serious losses incurred during the Battle of the Somme.

Short Bomber (9315)

Short Bombers were built by Short themselves as well as Mann Egerton, Parnall, Phoenix, and Sunbeam (who fitted their own 165kW (225hp) engine instead of the usual Rolls-Royce). 9315 was built by Short and was one of the aircraft transferred to the RFC in July 1916.

Short Bomber

Weight (Maximum take-off): 3084kg (6800lb)
Dimensions: Length 13.72m (45ft), Wingspan 25.6m (84ft), Height 4.57m (15ft)
Powerplant: one 190kW (250hp) Rolls-Royce V-12 liquid-cooled piston engine
Maximum speed: 124km/h (77mph)
Endurance: six hours
Ceiling: 3200m (10,600ft)
Crew: two
Armament: one 7.7mm (0.303in) Lewis machine gun flexibly mounted in rear cockpit; up to 408kg (896lb) bombload

Martinsyde Elephant

Though designed as an escort fighter, the ungainly Martinsyde G.100 instead found its niche as a bomber and was further developed into the more powerful G.102, capable of carrying a heavier bombload.

First flown during the autumn of 1915, the Martinsyde G.100 was nicknamed (semi-officially) 'Elephant' due to its unusually large size for a single-seat fighter. The G.100's large proportions were due to the requirement that it have a decent range, and the aircraft carried enough fuel to sustain a five-and-a-half-hour endurance.

Armament and range

Armed with a single Lewis gun on a mount above the top wing, some G.100s added a second Lewis gun immediately aft of the pilot's cockpit, firing rearwards, intended to be aimed and fired by the pilot, although it is unclear how he would manage to achieve this with any sort of accuracy whilst simultaneously flying the aircraft even in straight and level flight, let alone in the midst of combat.

The G.100's excellent range and weightlifting ability led to a gradual switch to the bombing role, in which it proved to be quite successful, though fighter patrols continued to be flown by the type until it became completely outclassed. Initially issued piecemeal to two-seater squadrons, only No.27 Squadron RFC was ever completely equipped with the type, and it was this unit that flew the G.100's first bombing mission when six Elephants bombed Bapaume on 1 July 1916, the first day of the Somme offensive.

A switch to a more powerful engine resulted in the externally near-identical G.102, again nicknamed Elephant, which was capable of slightly greater speed as well as carrying a somewhat greater payload, though at the expense of both endurance and reliability.

One hundred G.100s and 171 G.102s were built in total, and the G.102 served until the end of the war, with training units and in the front line in Mesopotamia.

Martinsyde G.100 Elephant
Weight (Maximum take-off): 1100kg (2424lb)
Dimensions: Length 8.08m (26ft 6in), Wingspan 11.58m (38ft), Height 2.95m (9ft 8in)
Powerplant: one 89kW (120hp) Beardmore 120hp six-cylinder liquid-cooled piston engine
Maximum speed: 154km/h (96mph)
Endurance: 5 hours 30 minutes
Ceiling: 4300m (14,000ft)
Crew: one
Armament: one 7.7mm (0.303in) Lewis machine gun fixed, forward-firing above wing and one 7.7mm (0.303in) Lewis gun fixed, firing rearward on the rear fuselage, just aft of cockpit on the port side; up to 120kg (260lb) bombload

---

This aircraft, serial no. 4735, was the prototype Martinsyde G.100 and is pictured here during testing at Martlesham Heath. A well proportioned machine, the G.100's performance never lived up to its looks and was, at best, adequate.

BOMBERS

Airco DH.4

One of the most successful aircraft of the war, the DH.4 was widely considered the best bomber of the conflict, was built in truly huge numbers, and enjoyed a long postwar career as a civil aircraft well into the 1930s.

Airco DH.4
Shortages of Rolls-Royce Eagle engines saw some DH.4s built with alternative powerplants. A8043 was one of a batch produced by Airco with the RAF 3a engine and was assigned to No.18 Squadron RFC but was shot down by ace Harald Auffarth on 16 March 1918.

Designed by Geoffrey de Havilland, the DH.4 was the aircraft that, above all, cemented his reputation as a designer. Faster than any fighter type to see service during the war but with excellent handling and an outstanding climb rate, the type enjoyed an enviable career in its intended role as a daylight bomber but also performed important work as a maritime patrol craft, an anti-Zeppelin interceptor, and later served as a high-speed transport aircraft.

First flight

Built in response to an official request for an aeroplane to be used for daylight bombing, and the first British aircraft specifically designed for this purpose, the first DH.4 appeared in 1916, making its first flight in August of that year powered by the prototype of a new engine design, the promising 170kW (230hp) 'BHP' (Beardmore Halford Pullin). Evaluation at the Central Flying School later in that year revealed that the DH.4 possessed excellent handling qualities and performance beyond that of any previous aircraft. Unfortunately, it was becoming clear that the BHP engine would not be entering production in its then-current form, and an alternative power unit was sought.

Luckily for the DH.4 programme, Rolls-Royce had developed its first aero engine, the Eagle, which happened to be of a similar power output and size and had recently entered production. Accordingly, a second DH.4 prototype was built and fitted with an Eagle, and it again demonstrated excellent performance. Consequently, orders for production aircraft, initially to be powered by the Rolls-Royce Eagle III, were placed by both the RFC and RNAS in late 1916.

Later production aircraft would utilize a wide variety of engines due to

Airco DH.4
Weight (Maximum take-off): 1575kg (3472lb)
Dimensions: Length 9.35m (30ft 8in), Wingspan 13.21m (43ft 4in), Height 3.35m (11ft)
Powerplant: one 280kW (375hp) Rolls-Royce Eagle VIII V-12 liquid-cooled piston engine
Maximum speed: 230km/h (143mph)
Endurance: 3 hours 45 minutes
Ceiling: 6700m (22,000ft)
Crew: two
Armament: one 7.7mm (0.303in) Vickers machine gun 7.7mm) fixed firing forward in the fuselage nose and one or two 7.7mm (0.303in) Lewis machine guns flexibly mounted in rear cockpit; up to 210kg (460lb) bombload

BOMBERS

ongoing shortages in Eagle deliveries, including units from FIAT, and once its production issues had been solved, the BHP. However, the Rolls-Royce remained the engine of choice throughout the DH.4's service life.

Production and supply boost

The DH.4 entered service with No. 55 Squadron RFC in January 1917, and six RFC squadrons were equipped with it by the end of the year. Likewise, RNAS units began to receive the type in the spring of 1917. Production and supply of DH.4s to RFC units received a boost following the daylight Gotha bombing raids on London, which resulted in a near hysterical public and official desire to 'strike back'. It was because of this policy that 50 DH.4s ordered by Russia were diverted for RFC use, and ultimately Russia received no DH.4s due to the October Revolution (captured examples would later be employed by the Soviets, however). On operations, the DH.4 proved a great success – the aircraft flew fast and high enough even when carrying its bombload to operate without an escort, its performance offering it a fair degree of immunity from interception by enemy fighters. The Rolls-Royce engine was reliable, and the aircraft was well-liked due to being comparatively easy to fly.

The DH.4 was not completely flawless, however, as the gap between the pilot and observer's cockpits effectively precluded communication between the two, and though a speaking tube was provided, this was of little use in combat. Furthermore, the placement of the main fuel tank between the two crew caused a degree of consternation, it being

Airco DH.4
This Westland-built aircraft featured a built up Scarff ring and was on the strength of No. 5 Sqn RNAS, based at Dunkirk in early 1918.

Airco DH.4
This flamboyantly decorated DH.4 with lightning flash and nose-thumbing devil on the fin was allocated to No.2 Sqn RNAS in July 1917 which became 202 Squadron RAF in April 1918. This aircraft was shot down by ground fire on 18 October 1918 off Zeebrugge.

BOMBERS

widely believed that the aircraft was unusually prone to in-flight fires, and the aircraft acquired the morbid nickname of the 'Flaming Coffin'. In reality, the DH.4 appears to have been no more susceptible to fire than any of its contemporaries, but the adoption of wind-driven fuel pumps in place of the pressurized fuel system in 1917 did much to allay lingering concerns regarding the aircraft's flammability. It is notable that American DH.4 personnel were particularly vocal regarding the fire risk, and their aircraft did not receive the updated fuel system.

British usage

Whilst the RFC were busy using the DH.4 for tactical bombing, the RNAS saw fit to employ the aircraft on coastal patrol, continuing with these missions after the creation of the RAF in April 1918. RNAS/RAF DH.4s were also used on anti-Zeppelin duties, and on 5 August 1918, Squadron Commander Egbert Cadbury (of the chocolate manufacturing family) and his observer Captain (later Air Vice Marshall) Robert Leckie shot down the Zeppelin L 70, a particularly significant victory as this airship was carrying *Fregattenkapitän* Peter Strasser, head of the German Navy's airship service. Following this loss, no further Zeppelin raids would be launched on the British Isles. Later the

Armament
Most DH.4s featured a single forward firing machine gun for the pilot and either one or two further weapons for the observer. Most RNAS machines differed from the norm in providing twin machine guns for both observer and pilot.

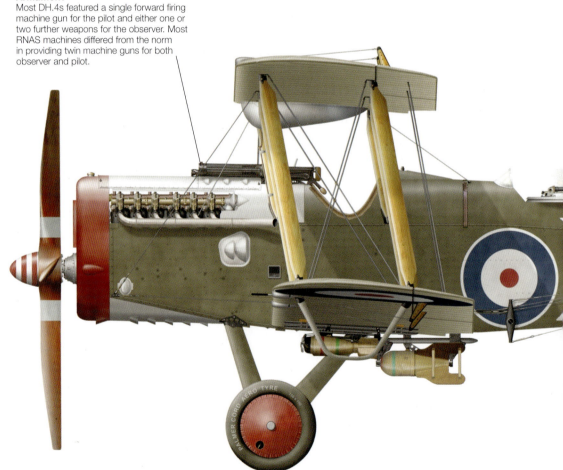

same month, four ex-Naval RAF DH.4s were jointly credited with the sinking of the German U-boat UB 12. British use of the DH.4 would decline after early 1918 as the (largely inferior) DH.9 began to enter service, but significant numbers of the bomber remained in service at the Armistice, with some subsequently being modified as fast passenger aircraft and used amongst other duties to regularly transport Prime Minister David Lloyd George from Westminster to the Versailles treaty talks in Paris, which was believed to be the first such use of an aircraft by a head of government.

Liberty Plane

In 1918, the second major user and producer of the DH.4 began operations on the type as the aircraft had been selected by the USAAS for licence production, US-built aircraft using the 300kW (400hp) Liberty L-12 engine,

---

Airco DH.4

Weight (Maximum take-off): 1575kg (3472lb)
Dimensions: Length 9.35m (30ft 8in), Wingspan 13.21m (43ft 4in), Height 3.35m (11ft)
Powerplant: one 280kW (375hp) Rolls-Royce Eagle VIII V-12 liquid-cooled piston engine
Maximum speed: 230km/h (143mph)
Endurance: 3 hours 45 minutes
Ceiling: 6700m (22,000ft)
Crew: two
Armament: one 7.7mm (0.303in) Vickers machine gun 7.7mm) fixed firing forward in the fuselage nose and one or two 7.7mm (0.303in) Lewis machine guns flexibly mounted in rear cockpit; up to 210kg (460lb) bombload

---

Tail
The DH.4s of No. 5 Sqn RNAS were unusual in that they featured the tricolor striping on the elevators as well as the rudder, leading to a very colourful tail unit. The 5 Sqn aircraft pictured on page 91 also has this distinctive feature.

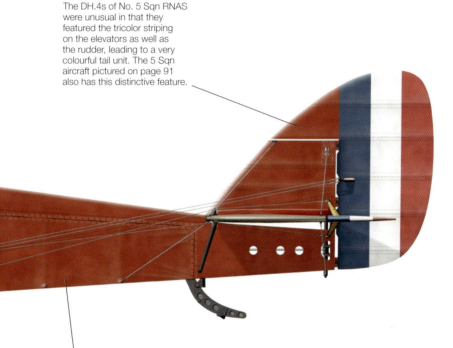

Rear fuselage
The fuselage of this DH.4 was unusual in that the sides were built up vertically and the top of the rear fuselage was flat. As can be seen, this entire area was painted in the flight colour, red.

Airco DH.4

A Westland built DH.4, this aircraft flew with No.5 Sqn RNAS. British bombing aircraft were not allocated to particular crews but this DH.4 was regularly flown by Flight Commander (later Squadron Leader) Charles Bartlett who served in the RAF until 1932.

BOMBERS

though despite the greater power of this engine, performance was actually inferior to the Rolls-Royce powered aircraft due to the Liberty's greater weight. The first American-built DH-4 was delivered to France in May 1918, with combat operations commencing in August 1918 and thirteen squadrons equipped with the type by the end of 1918. Known as the 'Liberty Plane', the US DH.4s saw intense action for the few months they were active, and four of the six Medals of Honor received by US aircrew were awarded to DH.4 crews. Two of these were won by Second Lieutenant Ralph Talbot and Gunnery Sergeant Robert G. Robinson of the US Marine Corps for managing to repel 12 German fighters that intercepted their aircraft during a bombing raid over Belgium on 8 October 1918.

The industrial might of the USA saw an amazing total of 4846 aircraft built in America, compared to 1449 in the United Kingdom, with manufacturers including the Boeing Airplane Corporation, the Dayton-Wright Company, the Fisher Body Corporation, and the Standard Aircraft Corporation amongst others. The DH.4 remained in service with the USAAC until 1932, and its availability, reasonable size, and decent performance saw it used for many experimental and testbed purposes. For example, the first trials of air-to-air refuelling were made with DH.4s in June 1923, with one such aircraft remaining aloft for 37 hours and 15 minutes on 27–28 August, during which it was refuelled in flight 16 times, setting 16 new world records for distance, speed, and duration. Five years later, Marine Corps DH.4s made the first US dive-bombing attacks in Nicaragua, and a few US Navy aircraft were modified into early casualty evacuation aircraft with provision for a single stretcher behind the pilot.

Surplus DH-4s were available cheaply and in large enough numbers in the US to be used for a vast swathe of tasks, such as surveying, photography, law enforcement, and agricultural applications. However, the best-known civil use of the DH.4 was as an airmail carrier. Adopted by the US Post Office as its standard aircraft in 1919, 100 DH.4s were modified to be flown from the rear cockpit with a 180kg (400lb) watertight mail compartment replacing the forward cockpit, remaining in service until 1927.

Airco DH.4
Weight (Maximum take-off): 1575kg (3472lb)
Dimensions: Length 9.35m (30ft 8in), Wingspan 13.21m (43ft 4in), Height 3.35m (11ft)
Powerplant: one 170kW (230hp) Siddeley Puma V-12 liquid-cooled piston engine
Maximum speed: 230km/h (143mph)
Endurance: 3 hours 45 minutes
Ceiling: 6700m (22,000ft)
Crew: two
Armament: one 7.7mm (0.303in) Vickers machine gun 7.7mm (0.303in) fixed firing forward in the fuselage nose and one or two 7.7mm (0.303in) Lewis machine guns flexibly mounted in rear cockpit; up to 210kg (460lb) bombload

Airco DH.4
One of a batch of Armstrong-Siddeley Puma powered DH.4s, which proved inferior to standard Eagle-powered aircraft, the strikingly marked N6416 named 'MOORQ' was operated by 2 Wing RNAS on Mudros during the Dardanelles campaign in January 1918.

94

BOMBERS

Airco DH.9 and DH.9A

The DH.9 was intended as a successor to the highly regarded DH.4 but proved inferior in almost every regard. A switch to the Liberty L-12 engine saw the problems rectified, and the DH.9A became a mainstay of the interwar RAF.

The DH.9's existence in large numbers derived from a 1917 plan to greatly increase the size of the RFC, with a particular emphasis on bomber squadrons; essentially a knee-jerk response to the daylight bombing of London earlier that year. As a result, large numbers of the outstanding DH.4 were ordered: a contract for 700 was placed on 28 June 1917, two weeks after the Gotha raid, but around a month later, drawings were shown of a modified DH.4 that promised greater range, designated the DH.9.

Hurried production

With a complacence that is probably attributable to the great success of the DH.4, and the fact that the DH.9 was a development of a current aircraft rather than a wholly new type, existing DH.4 contracts were switched to the DH.9 and vast new orders were hurriedly placed (at one stage totalling 4630 airframes), all before the aircraft had even flown. With the benefit of hindsight, this was a grave error, and by November 1917 both Hugh Trenchard, Commander of the RFC, and Sir Douglas Haig, Commander in Chief of the British Army in France, requested that production of the DH.9 be stopped. Nonetheless, despite its shortcomings, 4091 DH.9s would be built, and the aircraft was widely exported.

Design flaw and new problems

The first DH.9 (converted from a DH.4) flew for the first time in July 1917, featuring the wings and tail of the earlier aircraft married to a completely new fuselage and engine. The fuselage design eliminated the one major design flaw of the DH.4 by placing pilot and observer in close proximity and moving the main fuel tank to a position ahead

Airco DH.9
Weight (Maximum take-off): 1719kg (3790lb)
Dimensions: Length 9.27m (30ft 5in), Wingspan 12.92m (42ft 4in), Height 3.44m (11ft 4in)
Powerplant: one 170kW (230hp) Armstrong Siddeley Puma six-cylinder liquid-cooled piston engine
Maximum speed: 182km/h (113mph)
Endurance: 4 hours 30 minutes
Ceiling: 4700m (15,500ft)
Crew: two
Armament: one 7.7mm (0.303in) Vickers machine gun 7.7mm) fixed firing forward in the fuselage nose and one or two 7.7mm (0.303in) Lewis machine guns flexibly mounted in rear cockpit; up to 110kg (240lb) bombload

Arco DH.9

Another striking Airco, this DH.9 was built by Westland and served with No. 211 Sqn RAF. Despite being hit by ground fire and force landing as a direct result this aircraft survived to be used postwar as a trainer by the Dutch Army Air Force, retaining the striking markings.

95

BOMBERS

of the pilot's cockpit. The eradication of this problem resulted in the creation of a new one, however, as the pilot's visibility was significantly decreased, making reconnaissance difficult and rendering the aircraft incapable of nocturnal bombing due to the obstructed view and lack of visibility via the bombsight. But this issue was of little significance compared to the BHP-designed engine (produced in quantity as the Armstrong Siddeley Puma), which was unable to deliver its rated power and proved appallingly unreliable. As a result, the engine was derated to its production standard of 170kW (230hp) as opposed to the predicted 224kW (300hp), and the DH.9 could not meet its performance estimates, which had been notably optimistic even given the expected power of the engine. Unfortunately for RFC bomber units, mass production of the DH.9 was already under way, and the aircraft had to be used in service.

RFC usage

The first deliveries of production aircraft to the RFC occurred in November 1917, but the first unit to fly the DH.9

Airco DH.9

On the strength of No. 104 Sqn, a unit that had the dubious honour of forming with the DH.9 as its initial equipment in September 1917. No. 104 Sqn subsequently utilised the aircraft for the entirety of its operational existence during World War I.

Airco DH.9A

The DH.9A persisted in RAF service long after the end of the war. J7832 was on the strength of No.45 Sqn at Heliopolis in 1928 and has been fitted with an auxiliary radiator under the nose for desert operations.

BOMBERS

operationally was a naval squadron, No.6 Squadron RNAS, which flew the type's first mission in March 1918. In service use, the DH.9 suffered appalling losses. Without the speed or altitude performance of the DH.4, being a full 50km/h (30mph) slower than the older machine, the aircraft was unable to avoid interception by enemy fighters and had to fight its way to and from the target. Aircraft were frequently shot down, and desultory engine reliability led to many non-operational losses as well as countless instances of aircraft having to turn back due to engine trouble; for example, as late as 1 October 1918, 29 D.H.9s set out to bomb the railway junction at Aulnoye, but 15 had to turn back with engine trouble, and the mission was called off.

In various desperate attempts to improve the power of their aircraft crews resorted to unit-level modifications, such as enlarged carburetor air intakes and modified fuel mixture controls, but the losses continued; in a six-month period from May 1918 to the end of the war, Nos. 99 and 104 Squadrons had 54 of their DH.9s shot down and a further 94 aircraft written off due to accidents. However, it should be noted that the DH.9 was occasionally capable of impressive feats in the right hands and was quite capable of successfully engaging in aerial combat: on 23 August 1918 for example, Bermudian Lieutenant Arthur Spurling and his observer, Sergeant Frank Bell, single-handedly attacked thirty Fokker D.VII fighters, shooting down five of them, and Captain John Stevenson Stubbs achieved 11 victories in a DH.9, making him the leading 'ace' on the type.

Liberty L-12 saves the day

Once the engine situation became abundantly clear, various attempts were made to find a replacement. The Rolls-Royce Eagle of the DH.4 was required for the Bristol F.2b and was in short supply, so an alternative was sought resulting in a batch of DH.9s being built with the excellent 183kW (245hp) FIAT A.12, but production and delivery problems meant that engine could not be widely used. The new 300kW (430hp) Napier Lion was also considered but was at too early a stage of development (a Lion-engined DH.9 later set the world altitude record of 9300m (30,500ft) in January 1919), so attention fell instead on the American 298kW (400hp) Liberty L-12,

Airco DH.9A

This Airco built DH.9A was delivered to No.99 Squadron on 21 October 1918 and thus spent less than a month on operations. Like many of its kind it was used as an extemporised mail carrier in the immediate postwar period.

Airco DH.9A

Weight (Maximum take-off): 2107kg (4645lb)
Dimensions: Length 9.22m (30ft 3in), Wingspan 14.01m (45ft 11in), Height 3.45m (11ft 4in)
Powerplant: one 300kW (400hp) Liberty L-12A V-12 liquid-cooled piston engine
Maximum speed: 198km/h (123mph)
Endurance: 5 hours and 15 minutes
Ceiling: 5110m (16,750ft)
Crew: two
Armament: one 7.7mm (0.303in) Vickers machine gun 7.7mm) fixed firing forward in the fuselage nose and one or two 7.7mm (0.303in) Lewis machine guns flexibly mounted in rear cockpit; up to 340kg (740lb) bombload

BOMBERS

which was readily available due to the huge production effort in the US. Fitted with this heavy but powerful engine, performance of the DH.9 was transformed, and although never as fast as the speedy DH.4, the new engine was noted for its exceptional reliability, and the aircraft enjoyed a greater range and payload capacity than the earlier machine. Detail design work was carried out by the Westland Aircraft company as Airco had no spare capacity, and Westland became one of the major manufacturers of the type.

DH.9A

First flown in April 1918 with its new engine, the aircraft went into production as the DH.9A with No. 110 Squadron RAF becoming the first to equip with the type, flying their first bombing operations in mid-September 1918. A further three squadrons in France converted to the DH.9A in time to see action before the Armistice as well as some coastal patrol units based in the UK. Also operational in France on the type was the US Marine Corps' Northern Bombing Group, which flew the DH.9A operationally from September 1918

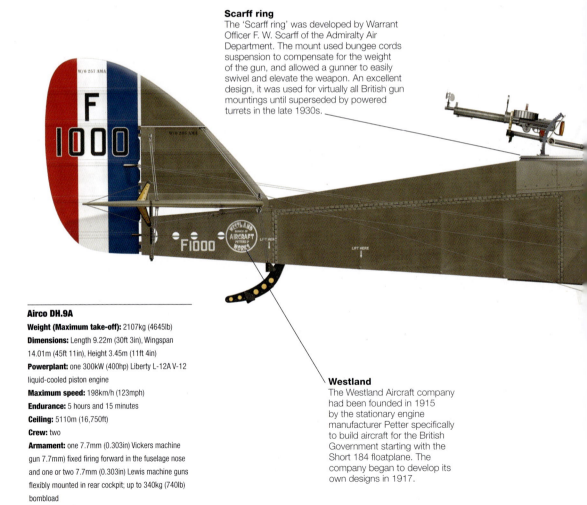

Scarff ring
The 'Scarff ring' was developed by Warrant Officer F. W. Scarff of the Admiralty Air Department. The mount used bungee cords suspension to compensate for the weight of the gun, and allowed a gunner to easily swivel and elevate the weapon. An excellent design, it was used for virtually all British gun mountings until superseded by powered turrets in the late 1930s.

Westland
The Westland Aircraft company had been founded in 1915 by the stationary engine manufacturer Petter specifically to build aircraft for the British Government starting with the Short 184 floatplane. The company began to develop its own designs in 1917.

Airco DH.9A
Weight (Maximum take-off): 2107kg (4645lb)
Dimensions: Length 9.22m (30ft 3in), Wingspan 14.01m (45ft 11in), Height 3.45m (11ft 4in)
Powerplant: one 300kW (400hp) Liberty L-12A V-12 liquid-cooled piston engine
Maximum speed: 198km/h (123mph)
Endurance: 5 hours and 15 minutes
Ceiling: 5110m (16,750ft)
Crew: two
Armament: one 7.7mm (0.303in) Vickers machine gun 7.7mm) fixed firing forward in the fuselage nose and one or two 7.7mm (0.303in) Lewis machine guns flexibly mounted in rear cockpit; up to 340kg (740lb) bombload

BOMBERS

Airco DH.9A
Built, like many Airco designs, by Westland, this DH.9A was supplied to No. 110 Sqn RAF in August 1918. Transferred to 99 Sqn immediately after the end of hostilities, it was written off in a landing accident while delivering mail.

Liberty engine
The DH.9A was powered by the American 'Liberty' engine, a V-12 unit that had been designed in five days by Jesse G Vincent of Packard and Elbert Hall of the Hall Scott Motor company. Time was saved by copying wholesale the valvetrain design of the German Mercedes D.IIIa.

Bombload
Like virtually all World War I bombers, the DH.9A carried its offensive armament externally. This example is carrying the standard RFC 104 kg (230lb) bomb, one of the heavier bombs of its era, designed for use against buildings, roads, and railways.

Presentation aircraft
Like many other aircraft, this DH.9A is a presentation aircraft, paid for by a donor, in this case Mir Osman Ali Khan, the Nazim of Hyderabad, who paid for 16 other British aircraft. Khan was, for a time, believed to be the wealthiest man in the world.

BOMBERS

to the end of the conflict. 885 DH.9As were built in Britain before the end of the war and, unusually, the majority of those still on order at war's end were also completed as the aircraft had been selected to be the peacetime RAF's standard light bomber, bringing the total produced up to 1730 in the United Kingdom. Large production contracts had been placed in the US totalling 4000 of an Americanized version designated USD-9A, but the end of hostilities saw only nine aircraft actually built.

By contrast, DH.9As abandoned by the RAF following the British intervention in the Russian Civil War were reverse-engineered and put into production as the Polikarpov R-1 in the Soviet Union subsequently over 2000 were built from 1924 onwards and used in action against Chinese forces during the late 1920s.

Postwar use

Much use was made of the DH.9A by the RAF after 1918, with aircraft remaining in frontline service until 1931, and it became particularly well known for its service in the Middle East and Central Asia, being called upon to occasionally bomb villages and camps of rebellious groups in Waziristan (now a part of Pakistan) and Afghanistan. An additional radiator was fitted under the fuselage to cope with the high temperatures encountered in that theatre, while water containers and spares, such as spare wheels and propellers lashed to the fuselage, were carried in case the aircraft were forced down in the desert. The Liberty engine was particularly noted for its reliability in this harsh environment, and the 'Ninak' was a popular, dependable machine. Budgetary constraints also saw the aircraft used as the basis for 'new' types, the Westland Walrus, for example, was a mid-1920s Napier Lion-powered fleet spotter aircraft which was simply a modified DH.9A, and the mass-produced Westland Wapiti of 1927 was a general-purpose aircraft which utilized the wings and tail of the DH.9A. The Wapiti, and its developed version the Wallace, later achieved fame for making the first flight over Mount Everest in 1933 and survived in service long enough to see combat in World War II.

The DH.9A became a stalwart of the interwar RAF, famed for its rugged airframe and mechanical reliability, particularly in the Middle East. This aircraft, E960, served with 39 Sqn in the UK before being transferred to 84 Sqn based at Shaibah in Iraq.

Sopwith T.1 Cuckoo

Although it entered service in 1918, the Cuckoo was just too late to be used in action during World War I, but the design was highly significant as it was the world's first landplane specifically designed for carrier operations.

Designated the T.1 by Sopwith, the Cuckoo originated in a request from Commodore Murray Sueter, the Royal Navy Air Department's Superintendent of Aircraft Construction, for a single-seat aircraft capable of delivering a 454kg (1000lb) torpedo and carrying sufficient fuel to provide an endurance of four hours.

Laying the egg

The Cuckoo (so named as it was intended to lay its 'egg' in other people's nests) was necessarily a large aircraft and possessed folding wings to simplify storage aboard ship. Sopwith had no experience with torpedo gear, so the necessary fittings and equipment required to carry and operate such a weapon were designed and produced by Blackburn, who had performed much experimental work in this area in concert with the RNAS. The prototype T.1 made its maiden flight in June 1917, and production aircraft were ordered from subcontractors Fairfield Shipbuilding Works in Glasgow and Pegler & Co Ltd (a pipe manufacturing firm). Neither company was familiar with aircraft construction, and delays ensued, with some of Pegler's order eventually being taken over by Blackburn.

Too late to serve

Enough production machines had been delivered by August 1918 for training to commence in the Firth of Forth, Cuckoos making torpedo attacks on targets towed by destroyers, and in November 1918, Cuckoos of No. 185 Squadron embarked on HMS *Argus* to begin operations, but the Armistice prevented any combat missions from being undertaken. Ninety aircraft had been built by the end of hostilities, but further production took the total number built to 232, and the Cuckoo remained in service until 1923. The aircraft was popular with pilots due to its strong construction, good handling and excellent ditching characteristics, the latter being important as the aircraft had no arresting gear and could not land on its carrier and was expected to return to a land base on completion of its mission, if possible, otherwise ditching at sea was inevitable.

Despite flying from ships, British naval aircraft were operated by the RAF between April 1918 and May 1939. This Cuckoo of the Torpedo Aeroplane School at East Fortune, Scotland was photographed dropping a Mk.IX torpedo in July 1918.

Sopwith T.1 Cuckoo
Weight (Maximum take-off): 1761kg (3883lb)
Dimensions: Length 8.69m (28ft 6in), Wingspan 14.25m (46ft 9in), Height 3.25m (10ft 8in)
Powerplant: one 150kW (200hp) Sunbeam Arab V-8 liquid-cooled piston engine
Maximum speed: 170km/h (106mph)
Range: 539km (335 miles)
Ceiling: 3700m (12,100ft)
Crew: one
Armament: one 457mm (18in) Mk.IX torpedo

BOMBERS

Blackburn Kangaroo

Although only 20 Kangaroos were constructed, the type made history by becoming the first aircraft to successfully attack a submerged submarine and the type proved effective and popular in service.

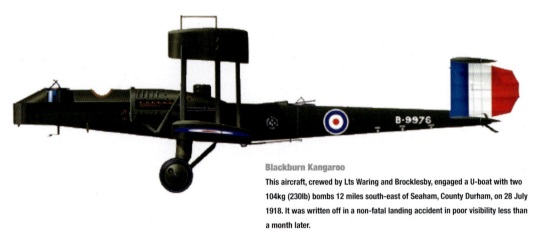

Blackburn Kangaroo
This aircraft, crewed by Lts Waring and Brocklesby, engaged a U-boat with two 104kg (230lb) bombs 12 miles south-east of Seaham, County Durham, on 28 July 1918. It was written off in a non-fatal landing accident in poor visibility less than a month later.

Derived from an earlier torpedo floatplane, Blackburn's R.T.1 (Reconnaissance Torpedo type 1) was built in accordance with the Air Board's increasing desire to use landplanes in the anti-submarine and convoy escort roles as unlike floatplanes, they were not dependent on favourable sea conditions for take-off and landing and tended to possess better performance.

The Kangaroo appeared in early 1918, and although 50 were originally ordered, tests revealed that the rear fuselage was prone to twisting and the aircraft suffering some control problems, and the order was cut to 20 (most of which were already in construction) despite the faults being eradicated in production machines and the aircraft's successful service use.

A world first
Delivered to No. 246 Squadron RAF in May 1918, the Kangaroos were used for coastal patrol for the remainder of the war. During one of these missions, one of the squadron's Kangaroos became the first aircraft to successfully attack a submerged submarine when, on 28 August 1918, the German U-boat UC.70 was spotted and crippled by a hydrostatically fused 236kg (520lb) light case bomb dropped by a Kangaroo, subsequently being sunk by depth charges from the destroyer HMS *Ouse*. Another four U-boats were damaged by the squadron in its six months or so of operations.

Airliner
After the war, the aircraft continued to be operated by 246 Sqn and were subsequently passed on to No 1 Marine Observers' School at Aldborough. Other Kangaroos were used as airliners, including three operated by Blackburn's own North Sea Aerial Navigation Co Ltd, and a single example was sold to the Peruvian military.

Blackburn R.T.1 Kangaroo
Weight (Maximum take-off): 3636kg (8017lb)
Dimensions: Length 13.46m (44ft 2in), Wingspan 22.81m (74ft 10in), Height 5.13m (16ft 10in)
Powerplant: two 190kW (250hp) Rolls-Royce Falcon II V-12 liquid-cooled piston engines
Maximum speed: 158km/h (98mph)
Endurance: 8 hours
Ceiling: 4000m (13,000ft)
Crew: three
Armament: one 7.7mm (0.303in) Lewis machine guns flexibly mounted in nose and dorsal positions; up to 417kg (920lb) bombload

Vickers Vimy

Only a handful of Vimys entered RAF service before the end of the war, but the aircraft achieved lasting fame after making the first non-stop flight across the Atlantic in 1919.

The Vimy owes its existence to the Gotha raid on London in July 1917, following which orders for new prototype bombers to retaliate against German targets were placed with Handley-Page and Vickers. The Vickers aircraft was designed by Rex Pierson, later to gain fame for the WWII Wellington bomber, and was designed to be able to strike targets in Germany itself, possessing sufficient range to bomb Berlin from bases in France.

Impressive machine

The first prototype made a great impression during its official evaluation at Martlesham Heath aerodrome, proving capable of taking off with a heavier payload than the Handley Page O/400 even though it possessed around half the horsepower of the Handley Page aircraft.

As a result of its excellent showing, contracts for 1000 aircraft were placed by the armistice, though most were cancelled, and only 112 would be built under wartime contract, though more Vimys would subsequently be constructed in the 1920s.

Long-distance flights

Too late to see active service in World War I, the Vimy formed the backbone of the RAF's heavy bomber force in the 1920s and was developed as both a military and civil transport, serving well into the 1930s. Several long-distance flights were made, including Keith and Ross Smith's journey from Hounslow Heath Aerodrome to Darwin in December 1919, but the most famous flight of all was the non-stop Atlantic crossing of James Alcock and Arthur Whitten-Brown in June 1919. Taking off from Newfoundland in a specially constructed Vimy with additional fuel tanks and a revised undercarriage, the Vimy crash landed in a peat bog in County Galway, Ireland 15 hours 57 minutes later. Despite appalling weather, the 3040-km (1890-mile) trip was completed at an average speed of 185km/h (115mph). The transatlantic Vimy is today preserved in the Science Museum in London.

Vickers Vimy I
Weight (Maximum take-off): 4937kg (10,884lb)
Dimensions: Length 13.28m (43ft 7in), Wingspan 20.75m (68ft 1in), Height 4.78m (15ft 8in)
Powerplant: two 220kW (300hp) Rolls-Royce Eagle VIII V-12 liquid-cooled piston engines
Maximum speed: 160km/h (100mph)
Range: 1400km (900 miles)
Ceiling: 2100m (7000ft)
Crew: three
Armament: one 7.7mm (0.303in) Lewis machine gun flexibly mounted in nose and dorsal positions; up to 1123kg (2476lb) bomb load

---

Vickers Vimy I

The Vimy FB.Mk.27A was sometimes referred to as the Vimy Mk.II and was intended for supply to the United States. H5066 was the second of an order for 75 Vimy Mk.IIs, later reduced to 25.

BOMBERS

Caudron G.4

A twin-engine development of the G.3, the Caudron G.4, like its forebear, was widely employed by several Allied nations. In British service, it was used by the RNAS for its nascent strategic bombing campaign.

Although a reliable and popular aircraft, the Caudron G.3 did not possess the power necessary to carry any meaningful bombload, and the crew nacelle was placed in such a position as to make the fitting of gun armament difficult. Therefore, whilst retaining the signature twin-boom layout of the G.3, Caudron simply doubled the power of the aircraft by fitting two Anzani engines to the G.4 rather than the single unit in the nose of the earlier aircraft, allowing a 100kg (220lb) bombload to be carried and for a position in the nose to be occupied by an observer/gunner with a trainable machine gun. Slightly greater in length and span, the new aircraft offered a significant improvement in performance, as was demonstrated in November 1916 when Italian pilot Guido Guidi set an absolute altitude world record of 7950m (26,083ft). Initially used by the French for bombing, the aircraft's excellent range meant it could reach targets in the Rhineland, though increasing losses saw it withdrawn from daylight missions in late 1916. Like the earlier G.3, the aircraft was widely used for reconnaissance as well as for bombing and saw extensive use with Italy and Russia as well as France.

RNAS role

British use of the G.4 was almost exclusive to the RNAS, which employed 55 examples as strategic bombing aircraft in the absence of any suitable British design. Twelve of the aircraft were built in the UK, and the remainder were supplied from France and used by Number 4 and 5 Wing of the RNAS to attack German seaplane and airship bases in Belgium throughout 1916, latterly accompanied by Sopwith 1½ Strutters. The Caudrons remained in RNAS service until the spring of 1917 when it was replaced by the vastly superior Handley Page O/100. One of their last major operations was against Bruges docks in February 1917 with No. 7 Naval Squadron.

Caudron G.4
Weight (Maximum take-off): 1890kg (2601lb)
Dimensions: Length 7.27m (23ft 10in), Wingspan 17.2m (56ft 5in), Height 2.6m (8ft 6in)
Powerplant: two 60kW (80hp) Le Rhône 9C 9-cylinder air-cooled rotary piston engines
Maximum speed: 124km/h (77mph)
Endurance: 3 hours 30 minutes
Ceiling: 4000m (13,000ft)
Crew: two
Armament: one 7.7mm (0.303in) Lewis machine gun flexibly mounted in nose; up to 113kg (250lb) bombload

This photograph is from a training slide for RNAS pilots and mechanics of the Caudron G.4 and shows off the aircraft's two Anzani ten-cylinder radials. Many other G.4s utilised a pair of lower powered Le Rhône 9C rotaries.

BOMBERS

Handley Page Type O

In 1914, Captain Murray Sueter, the director of the Air Department of the Royal Navy, famously asked for "a bloody paralyzer of an aircraft". The result of this request was the Handley Page Type O, the largest aircraft yet built in the United Kingdom.

The origins of the Type O stemmed from a series of meetings between the Royal Navy and Frederick Handley Page to discuss the potential design of an aircraft suitable for coastal patrol and dockyard defence that would also be capable of bombing the German High Seas Fleet at its home port of Kiel.

Origins and design
The RNAS initially favoured a seaplane design, but Handley Page managed to persuade them of the merits of an armoured landplane of unprecedented size, capable of carrying a 600lb bombload to be powered by two Rolls-Royce Eagle engines. The Admiralty approved the design in early 1915, and the aircraft made its first flight on 17 December. Designated O/100, 'O' being used as Handley Page used sequential letters to distinguish its aircraft types, and '100' referring to the wingspan in feet, the aircraft cemented Handley Page's reputation as a producer of large aircraft, a reputation it would retain for the rest of its existence as an independent aircraft manufacturer. So synonymous was the manufacturer with larger aircraft that for some years later, in Britain, any big aeroplane was popularly referred to as a 'Handley Page'.

Development of this first sizeable machine was not entirely trouble-free, however. The tailplane oscillated and twisted so severely that the rear fuselage was seriously damaged and required strengthening as a result. Though the root cause of the tail vibrations was eventually traced to resonance in the fuselage structure, which was relatively easily cured, locating the source of the problem had taken much time and effort. The aircraft also proved to be overweight, so nearly all of the armour was removed, and the enclosed cockpit was replaced with a more conventional open position.

Four O/100 prototypes were built, of which two were retained and brought up to production standard to act as training aircraft. In total, 46 O/100s were built before production switched to the O/400.

Handley Page O/100
Weight (Maximum take-off): 6060kg (13,360lb)
Dimensions: Length 19.16m (62ft 10in), Wingspan 30.48m (100ft), Height 6.7m (22ft)
Powerplant: two 190kW (260hp) Rolls-Royce Eagle II V-12 liquid-cooled piston engine
Maximum speed: 137km/h (85mph)
Range: 1100km (700 miles)
Ceiling: 2600m (8500ft)
Crew: four or five
Armament: two 7.7mm (0.303in) Lewis machine guns flexibly mounted in nose and dorsal positions and one Lewis machine gun flexibly mounted in ventral position; up to 910kg (2000lb) bombload

Handley Page O/100
This late production O/100 was delivered to Orford Ness military testing site where this experimental 'invisible' camouflage was applied. The aircraft went on to serve with No. 7 Sqn RNAS and later in its career the fuselage was repainted, though the wings retained this unique finish until the aircraft was written off in February 1918.

105

BOMBERS

The first 20 O/100s formed the equipment of Nos. 7 and 7A Squadron of the 5th Wing RNAS at Dunkirk and commenced operations in late 1916. Initial missions were flown in daylight and O/100s damaged a German destroyer on 23 April 1917, but the aircraft proved vulnerable to fighters, and a switch was made to nocturnal attacks later in the same month.

Most O/100 bombing sorties were undertaken by a solitary aircraft, and German-occupied Belgian ports, railway infrastructure, and airfields were the usual targets of these attacks, although the aircraft was also used for anti-submarine patrol as well.

One particularly busy O/100 was flown to the Greek island of Lemnos to attack Ottoman targets in support of the Gallipoli campaign. This aircraft was then intensively utilized to bomb a variety of targets over the course of 1917 before being used to supply Colonel T. E. Lawrence and the Arab Insurgency in September 1918.

Type O/400

By the time these operations were being carried out, however, production had moved on to an improved development of the Handley Page designated the O/400. There was little difference between the two aircraft, the major change being the use of 270kW (360hp) Eagle VIII engines in place of the 240kW (320hp) Eagle II units of the O/100. The O/100 had also used 'handed' engines with propellers that rotated in opposite directions, but the O/400 abandoned this feature in the name of improved simplicity and torque generated by the propeller was dealt with by simply offsetting the tail fin slightly. An increased bombload of up to 910kg (2000lb) could be carried and the airframe had been aerodynamically improved resulting in a higher top speed and ceiling. A total of 554 O/400s were built, including 107 under licence in the US (out of an order for 1500).

The O/400 started to arrive in France in April 1918, and the aircraft were worked hard bombing strategic targets. The O/400 was capable of carrying the new 750kg (1650lb) bomb and used this weapon in attacks on German industrial targets in such towns as Cologne, Mannheim and Wiesbaden. A raid on Kaiserslautern with heavy bombs and incendiaries on the night of 21/22 October caused 500,000 Marks worth of damage and on another occasion, a direct hit on an armaments store in Metz caused colossal destruction estimated by the Germans at over a million Marks. Although most operations saw no more than ten aircraft committed on any given night, the night bombing campaign reached a peak of activity on 14/15 September 1918 when no fewer than 40 O/400s set out to attack a variety of targets

Handley Page O/400

Built by the Metropolitan Railway Carriage and Wagon Company, this O/400 of No. 207 Sqn RAF based at Ligescourt is shown 'bombed up' with an example of the RAF's then largest weapon, the 748kg (1650lb) SN 1650 bomb, complete with graffiti.

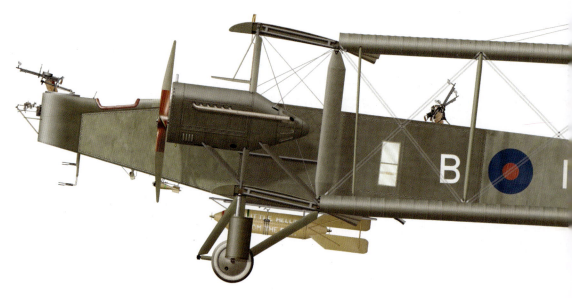

BOMBERS

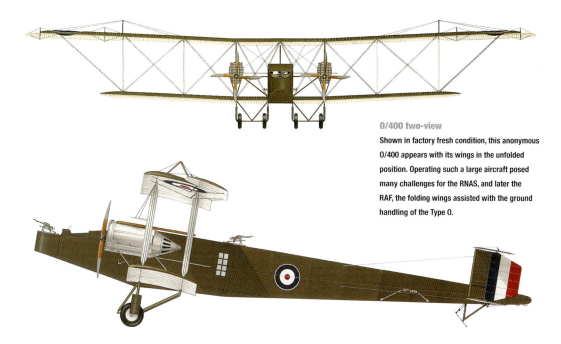

O/400 two-view

Shown in factory fresh condition, this anonymous O/400 appears with its wings in the unfolded position. Operating such a large aircraft posed many challenges for the RNAS, and later the RAF, the folding wings assisted with the ground handling of the Type O.

in Germany and occupied Belgium. In addition to strategic missions, the O/400s were regularly called upon to strike tactical targets, particularly against German aerodromes and communications targets.

Following the end of hostilities, the Handley Pages did not last long in service, being replaced by the Vickers Vimy in the peacetime RAF, though eight were converted as transports for diplomats travelling between London and Paris. Two of these were adapted for VIP use, finished in overall silver and named *Great Britain* and *Silver Star*. Twenty-five further O/400s were converted to airliners and continued for several years in civilian hands.

Handley Page O/400
Weight (Maximum take-off): 6060kg (13,360lb)
Dimensions: Length 19.16m (62ft 10in), Wingspan 30m (100ft), Height 6.7m (22ft)
Powerplant: two 270kW (360hp) Rolls-Royce Eagle VIII V-12 liquid-cooled piston engine
Maximum speed: 157km/h (98mph)
Range: 1100km (700 miles)
Ceiling: 2600m (8500ft)
Crew: four or five
Armament: two 7.7mm (0.303in) Lewis machine guns flexibly mounted in nose and dorsal positions and one Lewis machine gun flexibly mounted in ventral position; up to 910kg (2000lb) bombload

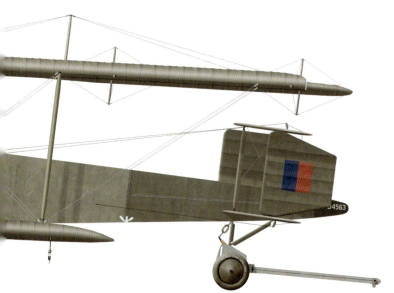

FLYING BOATS, SEAPLANES & AIRSHIPS

It is hardly surprising that the development of seaplanes and flying boats should be at the forefront of a nation whose power in the early twentieth century was profoundly derived from its navy. The development of large, long-range flying boats to combat the U-boat menace gave the British aviation industry a commanding lead in this area of development that was maintained throughout World War II and beyond.

This chapter includes the following aircraft:

- Short 'Folder' seaplanes
- Sopwith and Fairey Hamble Baby
- Fairey Campania
- Norman Thompson N.T.4
- Curtiss and Felixstowe flying boats
- Fairey III
- Beardmore W.B.III
- Airships

A Short 184 drops a torpedo during a practice mission. In August 1915 an aircraft of this type was the first to sink a ship by torpedo attack during the Gallipoli campaign, thus initiating a new form of naval warfare.

FLYING BOATS, SEAPLANES & AIRSHIPS

Short 'Folder' seaplanes

A diverse family of closely related aircraft, the Short floatplanes were built in large numbers and served effectively throughout the duration of the conflict. A Short 184 made history by becoming the first aircraft to sink an enemy vessel by torpedo attack.

The first of the 'Folder' types appeared in 1912, equipped with a patented wing folding system designed by Horace Short to minimize storage space, and the 'Folder' name soon became a generic term to describe a whole swathe of similar Short floatplanes. The first Folder was the Short S.41, which was successfully launched from the battleship Hibernia at the Fleet Review at Weymouth on 8 May. This aircraft was successful enough to prompt two further examples to be built, all three of which flew anti-submarine patrols following the outbreak of war.

S.81 and 166

Nine examples of the later S.81 were acquired by the Admiralty, and one of these became the first aircraft to drop a torpedo in tests held on 28 July 1914, although its range when carrying the weapon was so short as to be effectively useless if employed operationally. More powerful and useful was the Short Admiralty Type 166, which was intended for use aboard the seaplane carrier HMS *Ark Royal* and specifically designed from the outset as a torpedo bomber, although it was never used in that role.

Although only 26 examples of the 166 were built, the slightly later Sunbeam Nubian-powered Type 827 was built in quite substantial numbers, with 108 constructed. The most important member of the Folder family, however, was a follow on from the Type 166 design, the Type 184, of which 964 would be constructed, remaining in production from 1915 until the Armistice, such was its usefulness.

Short Type 184
Weight (Maximum take-off): 2433kg (5363lb)
Dimensions: Length 12.38m (40ft 8in), Wingspan 19.36m (63ft 6in), Height 4.11m (13ft 6in)
Powerplant: one 190kW (260hp) Sunbeam Maori V-12 liquid-cooled piston engine
Maximum speed: 142km/h (89mph)
Endurance: 2 hours 45 minutes
Ceiling: 2700m (9000ft)
Crew: two
Armament: one 7.7mm (0.303in) Lewis machine gun flexibly mounted in rear cockpit; up to 236kg (520lb) bombload or one 356mm (14in) torpedo

---

Short 184

The original Type 184, the aircraft's Type number deriving from this specific airframe's serial number, was used for development work before embarking, along with the second prototype, on HMS *Ben-my-Chree* and sailing for the Dardanelles and action in the Gallipoli campaign.

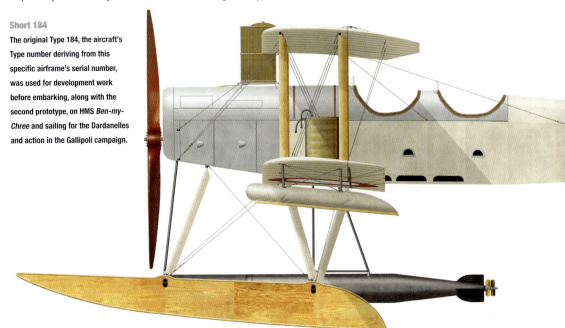

FLYING BOATS, SEAPLANES & AIRSHIPS

Evolution into Type 184

The first two prototypes were constructed in early 1915 and subsequently embarked upon HMS *Ben-my-Chree*, which sailed to Gallipoli in March 1915. On 17 August, Flight Commander Charles Edmonds used one of these aircraft to torpedo and sink a Turkish transport ship a few miles north of the Dardanelles, the first successful sinking of an enemy ship by an air-dropped torpedo. Remarkably, the second aircraft, flown by Flt Lt George Dacre, was forced by engine trouble to land on the water owing to engine trouble. Seeing an enemy tug nearby, Dacre taxied up to it, released his torpedo, and sunk it. With the weight of the torpedo removed, the aircraft was able to take off and fly back to the *Ben-My-Chree*.

Despite these successes, the performance of the Short 184 in the warm climate of the Dardanelles was, at best, marginal, the aircraft

This Type 827 was photographed whilst serving in German East Africa. This was probably one of those sent to Mombasa in July 1915 for operations against SMS *Königsberg* in the Rufiji delta.

was only able to carry a torpedo when the second crew member was left behind and a reduced fuel load carried. The Short floatplane was

therefore employed as a light bomber, carrying two 51kg (112lb) bombs, or for reconnaissance and gunnery spotting missions. Later, a Type 184 would be the sole aircraft to take part in the Battle of Jutland, but the vast majority of its service during the war was on anti-submarine patrols, and although many submarines were spotted and attacked, none resulted in a confirmed loss. Three hundred and fifteen remained in service in December 1918, and the aircraft served on in the RAF until all were withdrawn in 1922.

Back in 1917, however, the Type 184 was further developed into the larger Type 320, a slightly more powerful aircraft and superior torpedo-carrying machine, though as it turned out, the Type 320's sole intended torpedo attack was called off due to bad weather and the aircraft, like its predecessor was used as a reconnaissance seaplane until the end of the war. One hundred and twenty-seven Type 320s were built.

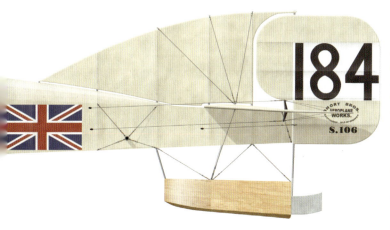

111

FLYING BOATS, SEAPLANES & AIRSHIPS

Sopwith and Fairey Hamble Baby

The Baby floatplane was developed from the Sopwith Schneider and was widely used as a shipborne reconnaissance and bombing aircraft from seaplane carriers and capital ships as well as from shore bases.

Fairey Hamble Baby
The first of 56 Fairey Hamble Babies built by Parnall, N1190 is seen here armed with both an unsynchronised Lewis gun and 51kg (112lb) bomb under the wing.

The ever-increasing amounts of equipment required to be carried by the Navy's scout floatplanes saw Sopwith replace the 75kW (100hp) Gnome of the Schneider with an 82kW (110hp) Clerget and later a 97kW (130hp) unit following yet further weight increases. Further changes included the adoption of a new cowling and an unsynchronized Lewis gun firing directly through the propeller arc, the reasoning being that it would be very rarely used, the majority of the bullets would pass through the propeller blades without hitting them, and each blade could take several hits before failure.

Sopwith Baby is born
The changes were deemed significant enough to warrant a name change, and the new aircraft became the

Believed to be N1194, this anonymous Hamble Baby is seen on the slipway at an unknown RNAS station, possibly Calshot. Note the Curtiss Large America moored in the background.

112

FLYING BOATS, SEAPLANES & AIRSHIPS

Sopwith Baby, making its maiden flight in September 1915 and entering service before the end of the year. Ultimately, 286 Babies were ordered for RNAS use, performing many functions, including flying patrols to provide early warning of approaching Zeppelin raids as far from Britain as possible. The aircraft also caught the attention of the Italian *Aviazione della Regia Marina*, and 100 were built under licence for Italian use by Ansaldo in Turin.

Fairey Aviation modifications

The Fairey Aviation Company took the opportunity to rebuild a standard Baby to incorporate a number of modifications when an example of the Sopwith aircraft was sent to the Fairey works for repair in the autumn of 1916, these proving successful enough to result in a production order. The most significant change was the addition of the Fairey Patent Camber Gear, a form of the now ubiquitous trailing edge flap used to increase lift for landing and take-off, the first such equipment fitted to a production aircraft. In addition, the span and planform of the wings were changed, and the tail surfaces were of a different shape to the Sopwith original. Entering service in mid-1917, Fairey Hamble Babies were operated by the RNAS in the UK, Mediterranean and Aegean on the same duties as their Sopwith forebears, carrying out anti-submarine patrols as well as engaging in occasional bombing missions. Of the 180 built, the last 74 were produced by Parnall as land planes and known as the Hamble Baby Convert.

Fairey Hamble Baby

One of the landplane Fairey Hamble Babies, the landplane variant simply utilised the same structure of struts that normally carried the floats but with skis and wheels fitted in their place, resulting in an abnormally wide track.

Fairey Hamble Baby

Weight (Maximum take-off): 883kg (1946lb)
Dimensions: Length 7.11m (23ft 4in), Wingspan 8.47m (27ft 9in), Height 2.9m (9ft 6in)
Powerplant: one 82kW (110hp) Clerget 9B 9-cylinder air-cooled rotary piston engine
Maximum speed: 148km/h (92mph)
Endurance: 2 hours
Ceiling: 2300m (7500ft)
Crew: one
Armament: one 7.7mm (0.303in) Lewis machine gun fixed forward firing on fuselage nose

113

FLYING BOATS, SEAPLANES & AIRSHIPS

Fairey Campania

Specifically designed to operate from the Royal Navy's seaplane carrier, HMS *Campania*, which gave the aircraft its name, this was the first totally original design from the Fairey company, and the first aeroplane designed to operate from a carrier.

The liner Campania was acquired by the Royal Navy in 1914 for conversion to a seaplane carrier, and the new Fairey seaplane was designed in 1916 with special regard to the hatchway dimensions and stowage capacity of the ship. The ship was fitted with a 461m (200ft) flight deck forward of the bridge by mid 1916 and floatplanes were launched from this structure using a wheeled dolly, subsequently being recovered by crane after alighting conventionally on the sea.

Prototype development and wartime history

Initially two prototypes were built, the F.16 with a 190kW Rolls-Royce Eagle IV engine and the F.17 with a 205kW (153hp) Eagle V, the first flying in February 1917. Both aircraft were subsequently used operationally from the Naval base at Scapa Flow. The F.17 was selected for production and 33 production aircraft were built followed by 27 examples of the 194kW (260hp) Sunbeam Maori-powered F.22. Most saw service on one of the three RN seaplane carriers, *Campania*, *Nairana* and *Pegasus*, though Campanias also operated from RNAS shore bases. In service the Fairey Campania proved dependable and delivered mostly unspectacular but useful service as a spotter aircraft.

The Campania's most intense action came as a result of British intervention in the Russian Civil War, the Nairana participated in one of the first combined air, sea, and land operation in history in the successful attack against the Bolshevik held fortifications on Modyugski Island in Northern Russia before scouting for Allied forces as they advanced on Arkhangelsk. The Campanias were subsequently stationed at Arkhangelsk for operations against the Soviets before moving to Kem in Russian Karelia to operate against White Finnish positions in the short-lived Republic of Uhtua in late 1918.

Fairey Campania

This Newhaven-based Campania was fitted with a huge experimental silencer above the top wing. In the pre-radar era the first warning of an approaching aircraft was often the sound of its engine and much experimental work was carried out attempting to eradicate noise.

Fairey Campania

Weight (Maximum take-off): 2417kg (5329lb)
Dimensions: Length 13.13m (43ft 1in), Wingspan 18.77m (61ft 7in), Height 4.6m (15ft 1in)
Powerplant: one 194kW (260hp) Sunbeam Maori V-12 liquid-cooled piston engine
Maximum speed: 137km/h (85mph)
Endurance: 4 hours 30 minutes
Ceiling: 1800m (6000ft)
Crew: two
Armament: one 7.7mm (0.303in) Lewis machine gun flexibly mounted in rear cockpit; up to 318kg (696lb) bombload

FLYING BOATS, SEAPLANES & AIRSHIPS

Norman Thompson N.T.4

Overshadowed by the more famous Felixstowe and Curtiss flying boats, and extremely obscure today, the Norman Thompson N.T.4 nonetheless delivered dependable service as a maritime patrol craft and served until the end of the conflict.

Norman Thompson N.T.4

Norman Thompson had worked with Glenn Curtiss and John Porte on the prewar Curtiss 'America' transatlantic flying boat and the influence of this aircraft on his later designs is obvious. N-2141 was delivered to RNAS Calshot on 26 November 1917, and is known to have served at Cattewater later that year before being struck off charge in June 1918.

The N.T.4 was developed by the Norman Thompson Flight Company from a flying boat it had built to enter the Daily Mail's 'Round Britain Race', which would have taken place in 1914 if war had not broken out. Ordered by the RNAS for maritime patrol use, by the time the N.T.4 entered service during 1916, it was often (and confusingly) referred to as an 'America', this having been adopted as a generic name for all large flying boats, regardless of their design, following the introduction of the Curtiss H-4. After the appearance of the H-12 'Large America', the N.T.4 was known, like the unrelated H-4, as the 'Small America'.

The first aircraft of the initial batch of six was experimentally fitted with a 40mm (1.57in) Davis two-pounder recoilless gun mounted above the cabin roof, though this was never used operationally.

Service history

Twenty-six N.T.4s were produced before production switched to the improved N.T.4a, of which 44 examples were built. The N.T.4A featured better cockpit glazing bestowing much improved visibility, and an engine change to the 149kW (200hp) Hispano Suiza improved performance.

The N.T.4As were initially utilized on anti-submarine patrol work but were gradually sidelined by the improved Felixstowe boats, in part due to their relatively lightly built hulls, and used instead for training until the end of the war. Two examples of a developed version, the N.2C, with an improved and strengthened hull, were built in 1918, but production did not go ahead due to the Armistice.

Norman Thompson N.T.4A
Weight (Maximum take-off): 2934kg (6469lb)
Dimensions: Length 12.65m (41ft 6in), Wingspan 23.95m (78ft 7in), Height 4.52m (14ft 10in)
Powerplant: two 149kW (200hp) Hispano-Suiza 8B V-8 liquid-cooled piston engines
Maximum speed: 153km/h (95mph)
Endurance: Six hours
Ceiling: 3600m (11,700ft)
Crew: four
Armament: one or two 7.7mm (0.303in) Lewis machine guns flexibly mounted in cockpit windows or on cabin roof; up to 209kg (460lb) bombload

115

FLYING BOATS, SEAPLANES & AIRSHIPS

Curtiss and Felixstowe flying boats

Effective and influential, the use of the large flying boats built by Curtiss, or derived from them, the only American-designed aircraft to fly in combat during World War I, cemented the flying boat's reputation as an invaluable maritime patrol asset.

The origin of this diverse family of related designs was the announcement in 1913 by the Daily Mail newspaper of a £10,000 prize for the first non-stop aerial crossing of the Atlantic. Glenn Curtiss and British Royal Naval pioneer pilot John Porte collaborated on a design capable of making the crossing, initially named the 'Wannamaker Flyer' after its sponsor but subsequently christened 'America'.

Early construction

Two prototypes were constructed and after early water-handling difficulties were cured by the addition of sponsons on the hull, the aircraft were designated the Curtiss H-2. The transatlantic flight attempt was scheduled to occur on 5 August 1914, but Britain declared war on the day before, and the attempt was postponed (permanently as it would transpire). Instead, Porte was recommissioned in the RNAS and encouraged the Navy to purchase the two America prototypes for further development as patrol aircraft, their great range making them ideal for such a task. Both were shipped to the United Kingdom following testing in September 1914 and were considered promising enough to prompt an order for a further H-2 as well as eleven examples of an improved version designated the H-4, four of the latter design being assembled in the UK by the boat-building company S.E. Saunders. In Royal Navy service, the aircraft were collectively referred to as 'America's' after the initial transatlantic craft and a further batch of 50 was ordered from Curtiss in March 1915. These craft were used for limited maritime patrol work from Felixstowe, and more extensively in the Mediterranean, but most of their service life was spent as training craft, in which they proved long-lived; at least three H-4s were still in service in June 1918.

Royal Navy service

Curtiss developed an enlarged version of the H-4, the H-8, which, though

---

Felixstowe F.2A

Weight (Maximum take-off): 4980kg (10,978lb)
Dimensions: Length 14.1m (46ft 3in), Wingspan 29.15m (95ft 8in), Height 5.34m (17ft 6in)
Powerplant: two 257kW (345hp) Rolls-Royce Eagle VIII V-12 liquid-cooled piston engines
Maximum speed: 154km/h (96mph)
Endurance: six hours
Ceiling: 2926m (9600ft)
Crew: four
Armament: one 7.7mm (0.303in) Lewis machine gun flexibly mounted at nose, dorsal and waist positions; up to 210kg (460lb) bombload

---

Felixstowe F.2A
Resplendent in 'dazzle' camouflage, N4545 also features an open cockpit configuration, believed to have been converted to this layout at Felixstowe whilst serving with No. 230 Squadron RAF.

FLYING BOATS, SEAPLANES & AIRSHIPS

Curtiss H-12A
Curtiss H-12 'Large America' in its original form. Spigot-mounted Lewis guns provided defensive armament but as can be seen, initially, all were mounted in the nose and cockpit area, and firing to the rear was hampered by the wings and engines.

Curtiss H-12A
Weight (Maximum take-off): 4831kg (10,650lb)
Dimensions: Length 14.17m (46ft 6in), Wingspan 28.26m (92ft 9in), Height 5.03m (16ft 6in)
Powerplant: two 205kW (275hp) Rolls-Royce Eagle I V-12 liquid-cooled piston engines
Maximum speed: 137km/h (85mph)
Endurance: 6 hours
Ceiling: 3300m (10,800ft)
Crew: four
Armament: one 7.7mm (0.303in) Lewis machine gun flexibly mounted at nose, dorsal and waist positions; up to 210kg (460lb) bombload

it remained a one-off, was also purchased by the Royal Navy and served as the basic pattern for the larger and more powerful H-12, which was built in quantity and used by both the British and US Navies. Originally powered by a pair of 118kW (160hp) Curtiss V-X-X engines, the H-12 was considered underpowered and was re-engined in Britain with two 205kW (275hp) Rolls-Royce Eagle I units, entering British service in this form, though the aircraft were later re-engined once again with 280kW (375hp) Eagle VIIIs. To distinguish them from the earlier H-4s, these boats became known as the 'Large America', as did the later H-16 development, which was powered by Liberty engines, the H-2 and H-4 retrospectively being referred to as the 'Small America'. In RNAS service, H-12s and H-16s operated from coastal flying boat stations on long-range anti-submarine and anti-Zeppelin patrols over the North Sea, proving effective in service and generally well-liked by crews. A total of 71 H-12s and 75 H-16s were acquired, commencing patrols in April 1917, with 18 H-12s and 30 H-16s remaining in service in October 1918. US Navy H-12s did not see service overseas, flying anti-submarine patrols from American naval stations. However, a few USN H-16s arrived in Britain in time to see limited service just before the Armistice, in the process becoming the only American-built aircraft flown operationally by American crews during World War I.

Porte's design
Meanwhile, John Porte had become commander of the naval air station at Felixstowe, Suffolk and instituted a series of improvements to the Curtiss H boats, which would see both the widespread modification of American-built aircraft as well as the production in the United Kingdom of new flying boats, derived from Curtiss to Porte's design, that would develop into the finest maritime aircraft developed by any nation during the conflict. Porte's efforts initially focussed on the H-4, which was criticized for its poor seakeeping and weak construction. A new hull, called the Porte I, was built of considerably greater strength than the Curtiss design whilst also incorporating much improved hydrodynamic qualities and married to the wings and tail of one of the second batch of H-4 boats. Featuring a deeper V-shape, two further steps were added to the hull during

Felixstowe F.2A
Built by SE Saunders, N4283 was delivered to Great Yarmouth Air Station in March 1918. This aircraft, flown by Captain Fitzrandolf, attacked a submarine on 17 May 1918 and was still listed as on strength at Yarmouth in January 1919.

tests, which greatly improved take-off and landing performance and led to the conversion of three further H-4 boats, which were redesignated as the Felixstowe F.1. More importantly, the success of this work saw Porte design a new hull for the more potent H-12 that would emerge as the Felixstowe F.2, and which was to prove staggeringly successful and influence flying boat design for years to come.

Pinnacle of design

The Curtiss H-12 was a much more capable flying boat than the H-4 but it shared the same problems of poor handling on the water and an overly weak hull. Fitted with a new two-step Porte II hull combined with the wings of the H-12 and a new tail, the first Felixstowe F.2 made its maiden flight in July 1916 and proved greatly superior to the Curtiss Large America on which it was based.

Following some structural modifications added in the light of operational experience with the first F.2, production of the new flying boat was authorized as the F.2A. Some later H-12s were also rebuilt with Porte hulls similar to that of the F.2A and were referred to as the 'Converted Large America'. One hundred and seventy-five examples of the F.2A were built by S.E. Saunders, May, Harden and May (both boat-building companies) and Airco, with the first production machines entering service during 1917.

This was just as the U-boat campaign was at its height, and between them, the F.2s and America boats sighted 67 U-boats and attacked 44 during that year. Three Zeppelins also fell to the guns of these aircraft during 1917, and the Curtiss and America boats would regularly clash with German floatplane fighters over the North Sea until the end of the war. The F.2A was not an easy target in aerial combat as it was both well-armed and surprisingly manoeuvrable for such a large aircraft.

The manoeuvrability and immense strength of the F.2A is ably demonstrated by the fact that one example is known to have performed a loop, a totally unprecedented manoeuvre for an aircraft of this size in the 1910s. Another example was landed in error on a ploughed field when the pilot misjudged his approach to Leeds reservoir, yet the only damage it suffered was a few (easily replaced) strained landing wires.

Final years

Further development resulted in the Felixstowe F.3; a slightly larger machine powered by two 239kW (329hp) Sunbeam Cossack engines. Despite possessing a greater range and heavier bombload than the F2, the F.3 was less popular due to its poorer speed and agility.

Despite the misgivings of its crews, the F.3 was widely used alongside the F.2A in the North Sea as well as in the Mediterranean between February 1918 and the war's end, with approximately 100 constructed, including 18 in Malta.

The final wartime development was the F.5, intended to incorporate the best aspects of F.2A and F.3, though, despite this, it actually possessed a performance inferior to both, though it was simpler to build than either. Post-war, the F.5 became the RAF's standard long-range flying boat and served until 1925 in the UK.

The wheel of development came full circle when the F.5 entered production in the USA in a specially adapted F.5L version, serving as the US Navy's standard patrol flying boat until 1928 and further developed in the US as the PN series, the last of which, the Keystone PK-1, was only retired in 1938. Coincidentally, the same year that the Japanese Navy retired its own F.5 development, the Hiro H1H.

FLYING BOATS, SEAPLANES & AIRSHIPS

Fairey III

One of very few aircraft to be used during both World War I and World War II, the Fairey III was a highly successful design that saw very widespread use during the interwar period.

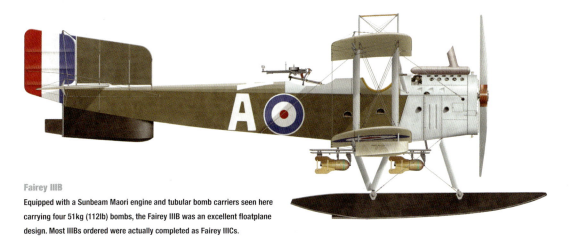

Fairey IIIB
Equipped with a Sunbeam Maori engine and tubular bomb carriers seen here carrying four 51kg (112lb) bombs, the Fairey IIIB was an excellent floatplane design. Most IIIBs ordered were actually completed as Fairey IIICs.

Intended from the start to be used as both a landplane and seaplane, the prototype Fairey III, then designated the N.10, flew for the first time in floatplane form in September 1917. It was later operated as a landplane, and once returned to Fairey following its evaluation, it was entered into the first postwar Schneider Trophy air race before being employed by Fairey for communications use until mid-1922.

Early production

The first production aircraft were 50 Fairey IIIAs, with a conventional wheeled undercarriage, which would enter RAF service in June 1918. The type was intended as a replacement for the RNAS's 1½ Strutters but saw little active service before the Armistice. The IIIB was the first floatplane variant, designed for bombing duties to the requirements of the Admiralty's N.2B specification, and sufficient numbers had been delivered for the type to have flown mine-spotting patrols from the seaplane base at Westgate-on-Sea in Kent in the weeks leading up to the Armistice. Two further squadrons were subsequently formed on the type at Felixstowe in Suffolk and Great Yarmouth on the Norfolk coast.

IIIC supremacy

The Fairey IIIC, however, did not see operational service during the war, the first being received at Great Yarmouth air station in November 1918. Combining the scouting role of the IIIA landplane with the bombing duties of the IIIB seaplane, it is widely regarded to have been the finest British seaplane designed during World War I. The type did however see active service during 1919 with the North Russian Expeditionary Force based at Archangel, where the IIICs were used to bomb

Fairey IIIB
Weight (Maximum take-off): 2219kg (4892lb)
Dimensions: Length 10.97m (36ft), Wingspan 19.13m (62ft 9in), Height 4.06m (13ft)
Powerplant: one 190kW (260hp) Sunbeam Maori V-12 liquid-cooled piston engine
Maximum speed: 154km/h (96mph)
Endurance: 4 hours 30 minutes
Ceiling: 3140m (10,300ft)
Crew: two
Armament: one 7.7mm (0.303in) Lewis machine gun flexibly mounted in rear cockpit; up to 315kg (690lb) bombload

Soviet naval vessels and attack rail communications during the Russian Civil War. Later the Fairey IIID and Napier Lion-powered Fairey IIIF were produced in large numbers during the 1920s, the latter variant remained in British frontline use until 1936 and was still being utilized as a target tug by the Royal Navy as late as 1941.

119

FLYING BOATS, SEAPLANES & AIRSHIPS

Beardmore W.B.III

Derived from the Sopwith Pup, the Beardmore W.B.III was a folding version specifically intended for use on the first of the Royal Navy's aircraft carriers.

Beardmore W.B.III
N6101 was fitted with jettisonable (non-folding) undercarriage and the mount may be seen to which the upward angled Lewis gun was fitted, the gun being arranged to protrude through a centre section cutout in the upper wing.

Beardmore produced Sopwith Pups under licence, so when a requirement arose for a shipboard variant of the Sopwith aircraft, they seemed a logical choice to modify the aircraft for such a task. Accordingly, Beardmore adapted the wings to fold backwards along the fuselage, resulting in the most obvious visual change to the design, as the pronounced forward stagger of the wings was eliminated to allow for both sets of wings to hinge at the rear spar and a second set of interplane struts was fitted just outboard of the fuselage. Though not as easily noticeable, the fuselage was lengthened so that the tailplane could clear the interplane struts when the wings were in the folded position, the tail itself being unchanged from the original Pup. An extended tailskid was fitted to allow the wingtips to clear the ground when folded. Flotation bags were fitted, and two undercarriage designs were used. The first featured a narrow track undercarriage that could be retracted into the fuselage, leaving the bottoms of the wheels poking out beneath the fuselage. The lower wings were fitted with skids to allow for the perceived loss of stability due to the new narrower track, but although undeniably ingenious, a more conventional undercarriage that could be jettisoned in the event the aircraft needed to ditch became the definitive design.

Production quantity

One hundred production machines were built, known to the Admiralty as the S.B.3 (for Sopwith-Beardmore 3, W.B.III was an internal Beardmore designation), and many saw service on Royal Navy ships. For example, 14 were assigned to HMS *Furious*, although they were not particularly popular as the alterations had markedly worsened the Pup's handling qualities, and the performance of the aircraft was soon exceeded by such types as the Ship's Camel. A few examples were supplied to the Japanese Navy, but all W.B.IIIs were withdrawn shortly after the Armistice.

Beardmore W.B.III
Weight (Maximum take-off): 585kg (1290lb)
Dimensions: Length 6.17m (20ft 3in), Wingspan 7.6m (25ft), Height 2.46m (8ft 1in)
Powerplant: one 60kW (80hp) Le Rhône 9C nine-cylinder air-cooled rotary piston engine
Maximum speed: 166km/h (103mph)
Endurance: 2 hours 45 minutes
Ceiling: 3800m (12,400ft)
Crew: one
Armament: one 7.62mm (0.303in) Lewis machine gun fixed firing forward on fuselage nose

FLYING BOATS, SEAPLANES & AIRSHIPS

Airships

Though not as famous as their Zeppelin contemporaries, several different types of British airship were used during World War I. The most successful were the Navy's non-rigid blimps, used for convoy escort and anti-submarine patrols.

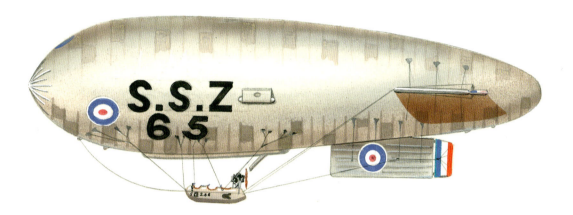

S.S.Z.65
One of the 77 strong Sea Scout Zero class, S.S.Z.65 survived the conflict to be withdrawn in 1919. It had spent over 254 hours in the air during the war.

British airship operations during World War I were exclusively the preserve of the Navy. The British Army had engaged in experiments with both rigid and non-rigid airships in the early years of the twentieth century, but in January 1914, divested itself of its remaining dirigibles, passing them on to the Navy.

Limited early usage
The Royal Navy had not made much use of airships beforehand, possibly due to the expensive and embarrassing loss of their first rigid airship in 1911; H.M.A.1 (His Majesty's Airship 1), nicknamed 'Mayfly', was never flown but was written off after a gust of wind broke it in two at its moorings. On the outbreak of war, the Navy possessed a motley collection of seven serviceable craft: one French-built Astra-Torres, one German Parseval, the four ex-Army ships, and a single airship built by Welsh pioneer Ernest Willows. A few patrol missions were flown with these aircraft, but airship operations were minimal until the introduction of the new SS class.

Submarine Scout beginnings
The declaration of unrestricted submarine warfare in British waters prompted the Admiralty to speculate that airships, with their excellent endurance and ability to reconnoitre large areas, might serve as a useful tool in the fight against U-boats and the 'Submarine Scout' or SS Class airship was developed as a result. The prototype SS class airship was a hurriedly cobbled-together lash-up consisting of nothing more than a B.E.2c fuselage and engine mated to the envelope of the old Willows airship. Ready for trials within a fortnight of

SSZ class airship
Useful lift: 605kg (1334lb)
Dimensions: Length 43.7m (143ft 5in), Diameter 9.1m (30ft)
Powerplant: one 56kW (75hp) Rolls-Royce Hawk six-cylinder liquid-cooled piston engine
Maximum speed: 85km/h (53mph)
Endurance (at full power): 50 hours
Ceiling: 1500m (5000ft)
Crew: three
Armament: one Lewis gun, flexibly mounted in the front cockpit; up to 110kg (250lb) bombload

121

FLYING BOATS, SEAPLANES & AIRSHIPS

An SS class blimp with B.E.2c fuselage RNAS airship returning to base after patrolling over the North Sea, ca. 1915.

type, so named because it featured a pusher design. Curiously, an SS Class airship still holds the altitude record for a British-built airship at 3100m (10,300ft), a record set in 1916.

Though highly successful, an airship with greater range than the SS Class was needed and an improved design with a more boat-like gondola was developed at the RNAS airship station at Capel-le-Ferne, designed by three serving naval airship officers. This became the first of the SSZ class, now featuring an extra crewmember and a 546 litre (120 gallon) fuel capacity, sufficient for an endurance of 17 hours, though most patrols lasted around eight hours.

However, much longer patrols could be flown – one of 50 hours and 55 min was flown by SSZ.39 in the summer of 1918. A rival design, the SSP, was also developed by RNAS Kingsnorth but proved inferior, and only six were built as compared to the 77 SSZs. In June 1918, a two-engined development, the SST class (T for Twin), was developed, of which 13 were built.

being given approval to proceed, the first SS Class blimp entered service in March 1915. A further 59 SS Class airships would follow it into service, which then spawned a variety of developed models.

Used for coastal patrols, 49 U-boats were sighted, 27 of which were then attacked by ships or from the air, but the SS Class, as with later blimps, proved most valuable as a deterrent; many German submarine commanders preferred not to risk an attack if an airship was in the area, as it could instantly report their position to escort vessels if they launched a torpedo. Three versions of SS Class blimps were built, the original version with a B.E.2c fuselage, the Armstrong Whitworth type, which utilized an F.K.3 fuselage for its gondola and the Maurice Farman

N.S.7

This airship had one of the longest careers of the N.S. class from May 1918 onwards, spending most of its operational life based at East Fortune in Scotland. After the war N.S.7 undertook trials with HMS *Furious*, alighting on the carrier for the first time on 7 July 1919.

FLYING BOATS, SEAPLANES & AIRSHIPS

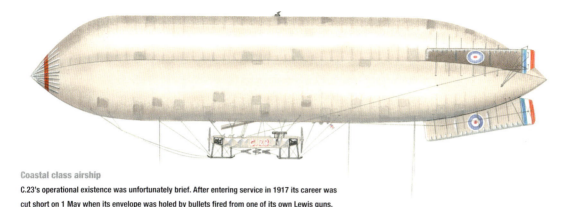

Coastal class airship
C.23's operational existence was unfortunately brief. After entering service in 1917 its career was cut short on 1 May when its envelope was holed by bullets fired from one of its own Lewis guns.

Coastal class

A separate branch of development resulted in the Coastal or C class. This was derived from the distinctive Astra-Torres trilobe envelope, under which was suspended a gondola with two engines mounted fore and aft. Larger than the SS Class, the Coastal blimps featured a crew of five and were the first British airships able to carry a meaningful bomb load with which to attack submarines, and a total of six U-boats were officially credited lost to C Class attacks. A defensive armament of between two and six Lewis guns was carried and the craft featured a gun position on top of the aircraft, accessible by a ladder in a vertical tube through the envelope. By the end of the war, the C Class was experimenting with an early form of ASDIC equipment mounted to a buoy lowered onto the water but the war ended before development was complete. Thirty-five C class blimps were built as well as a further 10 of the slightly larger C Star class. The last, largest, and best blimp design of the war, the North Sea or NS Class, originated in a need for yet greater endurance, heavier armament, and the ability to carry two complete crews to deal with patrols that might last days rather than hours.

The first convoy escort mission was flown in April 1918 by N.S.3 and lasted over 55 hours. Fourteen were built, of which six were in service at the Armistice, and the effectiveness of the RNAS blimps may be gauged by the fact that during 1918, no ship was lost to submarine attack from any convoy escorted by airships.

Lone engager

Rigid airship development also occurred in the UK, and the RNAS eventually operated several craft of this type, though most were used almost exclusively for training and experimental work. The only British rigid to actually engage in combat was R.29, one of two R.23x class airships, built with knowledge gleaned from Zeppelin L 33, which had force-landed virtually undamaged in Essex. R.29 was commissioned on 20 June 1918 and flew several patrols, encountering U-boats on three occasions. The last of these took place on 29 September 1918 when she attacked UB-115 off Northumberland. During the attack, R.29 dropped two 100kg (230lb) bombs and was joined by two destroyers and armed trawlers. The submarine was reported destroyed in the attack, becoming the only recorded victim of a British rigid airship.

Escorted by a C Star blimp, German battlecruisers steam towards internment in Scapa Flow, in the Orkney Islands, Scotland in November/December 1918. British naval airship operations did not continue for long after the war.

123

Index

Page numbers in **bold** refer to information contained in captions.

ABC Dragonfly engine 47
aces
    American 59
    Bermudian 97
    British 13, 14, 18, 41–2, 54, 56, 97
    Canadian **71**
    French 21
    German 30, 59, **90**
    'Gunbus' 56
    Imperial Russian 22
Admiralty 7, 46, 70, 88, 105, 110, 120–1
Aegean 113
aerial reconnaissance 6, 49, 51, 53, 65, 68, **68**, 71, 73, 81, 86, 87
Aéronautique Militaire 65
Afghanistan 100
Air Board 102
Airco 117
Airco DH.1 13, 57
Airco DH.2 13–14, **13**, **14**, 26, 27, 58
Airco DH.4 81, 85, **85**, 90–4, **90**–4, 95, 97, 98
Airco DH.5 26, **26**
Airco DH.9 93, 95–100, **95**–**6**
    Airco DH.9A 95–100, **96**–**100**
aircraft carriers 6–7, 11, 35–6, 70, 101, 110–11, 114
airships 109, 121–3, **121**–**3**
    see also Zeppelins
Albatros 27, 70
Albatros D.I. 23, **58**, 60
Albatros D.II. 23
Albatros D.III 27, 30, 33, 34, 80
Albatros D.V. 34, **80**
Alcock, James 103
Amiens, battle of 7
Ansaldo 113
Antwerp 10
Anzani engines 104
Arab Insurgency 106
Argentina 43
Argus (aircraft carrier) 101
Ark Royal (seaplane carrier) 110
Arkell, Lt A. J. **80**
Arkhangelsk (Archangel) 114, 119
Armstrong Siddeley Lynx engine 64
Armstrong Siddeley Puma engine **94**, 96
Armstrong Whitworth 122
Armstrong Whitworth F.K.3 ('Little Ack') 75–6, **75**, 78, 122
Armstrong Whitworth F.K.8 ('Big Ack') 74–8, **76**–**8**, 79, 81, 82

Arras 37
    second battle of 80
ASDIC 123
Astra-Torres 121, 122–3
Atkey, Lt Alfred 81
Atlantic crossings, non-stop 103, 116
Auffarth, Harald **90**
Aulnoye 97
Australia (battlecruiser) **49**
Australian Flying Corps 26
    No. 1 Sqn **79**
    No. 2 Sqn 26
    No. 4 Sqn 47
Austro-Daimler engines 68
Aviatik B.I 87
Aviation Militaire 71
Aviazone della Regia Marina 113
Avro 500 62
Avro 504 62–4
    Avro 504A **62**–**3**
    Avro 504J **63**, 64
    Avro 504K **63**, 64, **64**
    Avro 504N 64, 64
Avro Lancaster 85
Avro Tutor 64
Avro U-1 64

Baizieux, France 26
Baldwin, 2nd Lt **83**
Balkans 28, 75
Ball, Albert 41, 54
Bapaume 89
Barker, Maj William 34
Barker, W. G. **35**
Barker, William 47
Barling, Walter 72
Barnwell, Frank 11, 28, 79
Bartlett, Flt Cdr **93**
Beardmore 16, **51**, 57, **60**, 79
Beardmore Halford Pullin (BHP) engine 90–1, 96
Beardmore W.B.III 120, **120**
Beauchamp-Proctor, Andrew 41
Béchereau, Louis 31, 44
Belgium 24, 38, 74, 83, 94, 104, 106–7
Bell, Sgt Frank 97
Ben-my-Chree (seaplane carrier) 111
Berlin 7
Bishop, William Avery 'Billy' 18, 41
Blackburn 101
Blackburn R.T.1 Kangaroo 102, **102**
blind spots 26
Boeing Airplane Corporation 94
Bolsheviks 114
bombers 85–107
Boulton & Paul of Norwich **59**
Brazil 43
Breguet 14 71

Bricklesby, Lt **102**
Bristol Aircraft Company 28, 78
Bristol 'Bullet' *see* Bristol Scout
Bristol F.2 42, 74, 77–83
    Bristol F.2A 79–80, 81
    Bristol F.2B 49, **79**, 81–3, **81**, **83**, 97
    MK.II 82
    MK.III 82
    MK.IV 82
Bristol M.1 28
    Bristol M.1A 28
    Bristol M.1B 28
    Bristol M.1C 28, **29**
Bristol Scout 10, 11, 12, 58
    Bristol Scout C **11**
Bristol XB-1A 83
Bristol XB-1B 83
British Army 6–7, 11, 71, 85, 121
    see also Royal Flying Corps
British Expeditionary Force 6
Browning guns 83
Bruges docks 104
Bulgaria 75
Burton, 2nd Lt **57**
Busk, Edward 50–1

Cadbury, Sqn Cdr Egbert 92
Cambrai aerodrome 53
Campania (seaplane carrier) 114
Canadian pilots 18, 29, 30, 33, 39, 41, 42, 45, 47, 58, **71**, 81
Capel-le-Ferne 122
Carey, 2nd Lt A. S. **70**
Caudron 87
Caudron G.2 65
Caudron G.3 65, **65**, 104
    Caudron G.3 D2 65
    Caudron G.3 E2 65
    Caudron G.3 R1 65
Caudron G.4 70, 88, 104, **104**
Central Flying School **50**, 90
Challenger guns 22
Chile 43
China 61, 65, 100
Clerget engines 18, 22, 112
Coastal (C) class airships 122–3, **123**
Collishaw, Raymond 30, **71**
Cologne 10, 106
Comines railway station 61
Constance, Lake 63–4
Constantinesco synchronization gear 54, 78
Constantinesco-Colley synchronization gear ('C.C. Gear') 41
Cooper bombs **53**
Courtai railway station 61
Coventry Ordnance Works **73**
Cowan, Lt Sidney 13

Cunnell, Captain D. C. 60
Curtiss 42, 83
Curtiss, Glenn 116
Curtiss flying boat **109**, 115, 116–18
    Curtiss H-2 ('Small America') 116, 117
    Curtiss H-4 ('Small America') 115, 116–17
    Curtiss H-8 117
    Curtiss H-12 ('Large America') 115, 117
    Curtiss H-16 ('Large America') 117
Curtiss V-X-X 117

Dacre, Flt Lt George 111
Daily Mail (newspaper) 43, 62, 116
    'Round Britain Race' 115
Dalrymple, Capt Sydney **83**
Dardanelles campaign **87**, **94**, 111
Darracq, Paris **56**
Davis guns 115
Dayton-Wright Company 83, 94
de Havilland, Geoffrey 13, 26, 50, 57, 90
Delage, Gustave 16, 17
Denmark 36
Derfflinger (battlecruiser) **123**
Dowding, Major Hugh 54
Duffus, Major Chester Stairs **58**
Dunkirk 30, 106
Dusseldorf 10
Dutch Army Air Force **95**

Eberhart Aeroplane 42–3
Eberhart S.E.5e 43
Edmonds, Flt Cmr Charles 111
Emile Mayen 46
Epsom Derby 43
Estonia 38
Everest, Mount 100

Fairey Aviation Company 113
Fairey Campania 114, **114**
Fairey F.16 114
Fairey F.17 114
Fairey III 119
Fairey IIIA 119
Fairey IIIB 119, **119**
Fairey IIIC 119
Fairey IIID 119
Fairey IIIF 119
Fairey Patent Camber Gear 113
Fairfield Shipbuilding Works 101
Farman 71, 87
Farman MF.7 ('Longhorn') 86
Farman MF.11 ('Shorthorn') 59, 86, **86**
    Farman MF.11bis 86
Farnborough 11

INDEX

Felixstowe 119
Felixstowe flying boat 115, 116–18
   Felixstowe F.1 117
   Felixstowe F.2 **7**, 117
   Felixstowe F.2A **116**, 117–18, **118**
   Felixstowe F.3 118
   Felixstowe F.5 118
FIAT 91
FIAT A.12 97
Firth of Forth 101
Fisher Body Corporation 94
flying boats 109–20
Fokker 23
Fokker Dr.I 30, 78
Fokker D.VII 28, 37, 39, 47, 97
Fokker E.I 'Eindecker' 53
Fokker Eindecker 13, 15, 16, 56, 59
'Fokker Scourge' 16, 58–9
Folland Gnat jet trainer 39
Folland, Henry 39
France 6, 12–13, 18, 20, 27, 30, 32, 37, 40, 44–5, 50, 52, 54–5, 63, 65, 67, 68, 69, 70–1, 78–9, 81–2, 86–7, 94, 98, 103–4, 106
Frantz, Sergeant Joseph 87
French, General John 6
French forces 15
Fullard, Phillip 18
Furious (pioneer aircraft carrier) **6**, 7, 35–6, 70, 120

G & J Weir, Glasgow **57**
Gallipoli campaign 106, 111
Garros, Raymond 66
Gass, Lt. Charles 81
Georgia 38
German Air Service
   Jasta 2 **51**
   Jasta 11 80
   Jasta 12 **61**
German Army 38
   1st Army 6
German Navy 36, 92
   High Seas Fleet 105
German spring offensive March 1918 37–8
Germany 10, 17, 103, 107
Gille, Unteroffizier F. **61**
Gillet, Francis 46
Gloster Gladiator 39, 45
Gnôme engines **12**, 13, 64, 112
   Lambda 62
   Monosoupape 24, 55
Gontrode 52
Gooden, Major Frank 39
Gordon Bennett Cup 16
Gotha bombers 24, 54, **80**, 91, 95, 103
   Gotha G.IV 36
Great Yarmouth 119
Greece 30, 38, 78, 106
Green engines 57

Griffiths, 2nd Lt F. W. **57**
Guidi, Guido 104

Haig, Sir Douglas 95
Halberstadt 23
Hammond, Lt A. W. 78
Handley, 2nd Lt F. A. W. **61**
Handley Page 103
Handley Page, Frederick 105
Handley Page Halifax 85
Handley Page Type O 105–7
   Handley Page Type O/100 88, 104, 105–6, **105**
   Handley Page Type O/400 85, 103, 105, 106–7, **106**, 106–**7**
Handley Page V/1500 7
Hargreaves, James McKinley 55–6
Hawker, Harry 23, 29–30, 45
Hawker, Maj (formerly Lt) Lanoe 11, 52
Heckscher, G. M. **109**
Hewlett & Blondeau **50**, **75**
Hibernia (battleship) 110
Hindenburg (battlecruiser) **123**
Hiro H1H 118
Hispano-Suiza 42, 53, 74, 79, 83, 115
   Hispano-Suiza 8 engine 31, 39, 40, 44–6
   Hispano-Suiza E engine 43
   Hispano-Suiza HS.8B engine 46
H.M.A.1 (His Majesty's Airship 1) 121
Home Defence units 14, 15, 22, 24, **52**, 54, 64, **64**, 70
Horrell, Capt Frederick **81**
Horsfall, Capt 53

Il-2 Sturmovik 7
Imbros **87**
Immelman, Hans **51**
Immelman, Max 59
Imperial Gift 1919 **81**
Ireland 43
Italy 17, **35**, 44, **80**, 86–7, 104

Japanese forces 86
Japanese Navy 43, 118, 120
Jutland, battle of 111

Kaiserin Elisabeth (German cruiser) 86
Kaiserslautern 106
Kellner Frères 44
Kem 114
Kenworthy, John 27, 39, 72
Keystone PK-1 118
Kiel 105
Kluck, Alexander von 6
Koolhoven, Frederick 75, 76
Kut 12

Langan-Byrne, Patrick 14
Latvia 38
Lawrence, Col T. E. 106
Le Prieur rockets **52**
Le Rhône engines 15, 19, 66, 67
   9J 16
Leckie, Capt Robert 92
Lemnos 106
Lewis guns 10, 12, 16–17, 20, 35–6, 41, 45–6, **52**–**3**, 54, **56**, 57, 64, **64**, 67, 69–70, 78, 81, 89, 112, 123
Libby, Capt Frederick 59
Liberty L-12 engine 83, 93–5, 97–8, **99**, 100, 117
'Liberty Plane' (American DH-4) 94
Liddell, Capt J. A. **68**
Lloyd George, David 93
London 91
   air raids 24, 95, 103
   East **80**
London-Paris-London race 11
Low, Archie 55

MacArthur, Capt L.W. **70**
Macedonia 22, 78
Malta 118
Mann Egerton 32, **88**
Mannheim 106
Mannock, Edward 'Mick' 18, 41
Marlin guns 83
Martin & Handasyde company 12
Martinsyde F.4 Buzzard 47
Martinsyde G.100 Elephant 89, **89**
Martinsyde G.102 Elephant 89
Martinsyde Scout 1 (S.1) 12, **12**
Maurice Farman 122
Maxim guns 57
May, Harden and May 117
McCudden, James 42
McKeever, Maj Andrew 81
Mediterranean 70, 113, 116, 118
Menin railway station 61
Mesopotamia 12, 32, 89
Messines, battle of 27
Metropolitan Railway Carriage and Wagon Company **106**
Metz 106
Middle East 22, 28, 32, 65, 100, **100**
Military Cross 78
Mir Osman Ali Khan, Nazim of Hyderabad **99**
McLeod, 2nd Lt Alan A. 78
Modyugski Island 114
Moltke (battlecruiser) **123**
Mons 6
Morane-Saulnier Type L 66, **66**
   Morane-Saulnier Type LA 66
Morane-Saulnier Type N 15, **15**
Morane-Saulnier Type P 66, 67
Morane-Saulnier BB 67, **67**
Moslains 37
Mouveaux aerodrome 61
MS.24 engine 66

Mudros **94**
Muller, Leutnant Max von **70**
Murlis Green, Gilbert 36, 37

Nairana (seaplane carrier) 114
Napier Lion 97, 100, 119
Naval Aircraft Factory PN 118
Netherlands 38
New Zealand **81**
Nicaragua 94
Nieuport 10 16
Nieuport 11 ('Bebe') 15, 16, 17
Nieuport 12 16
Nieuport 16 16, **16**, 17
Nieuport 17 17–18, **17**, 21, 27, 33, 40
   Nieuport 17bis 18, 20
Nieuport 21 17, 18
Nieuport 23 17, 18, **19**
   Nieuport 23bis 18
Nieuport 24 18, 20–1
Nieuport 27 18, 20–1, **20**, **21**
Nieuport & General Aircraft Company Ltd 17, 18, 31
Nieuport Scout 9, 14, 18, 20, 21, 58
   Early 16, **16**
night missions 36–7, **58**, 60–1, 64, **64**, **80**, 86
No. 1 Marine Observers' School, Aldborough 102
No. 2 Aircraft Depot **76**
Norman Thompson Flight Company 115
Norman Thompson N.2C 115
Norman Thompson N.T.4 (the 'Small America') 115, **115**
North Russian Expeditionary Force 119
North Sea 117, 118
North Sea Aerial Navigation Co Ltd 102
North Sea (NS) class airships **122**, 123
Nungesser, Charles 21

Oades, Lt Sydney **80**
October Revolution 91
Offoy 37
O'Gorman, Mervyn 50
Olympia Aero Show 55
Orford Ness **105**
Ostend 88
Ottoman forces 106
Ouse (destroyer) 102

Palestine 14, 20, 22, 78, **79**
Paraguayan revolution 1922 78
Parliament 53
Parnall **88**, 113
Parseval 121
Passchendaele, battle of 61
Peck, Lt **68**
Pegasus (seaplane carrier) 114

125

INDEX

Pegler & Co Ltd 101
Pemberton-Billing, Noel 53
Percival, 2nd Lt E. **61**
Pershing, General John J. 83
Phoenix **88**
Pierson, Rex 103
Pithey, Lt Croye 74
Poland 38, 43, 83
Polikarpov Po-2 64
Polikarpov R-1 100
Polish-Soviet War 83
Porte, John 116, 117
Powell, Lt Leslie 81

Queensland and Northern Territory Aerial Services (QANTAS) 78
Quénault, Cpl Louis 87

R.23x class airship 123
R.29 class airship 123
Rabagliati, Lt Euan 63
Rameshwar Singh, Maharaja **80**
Ranken darts 11
Rees, Lionel 55–6
Reid, Lewis **81**
Renault engines 50, 52, 75
Repulse (battlecruiser) 70
Rhodes, Hervey 74
Richthofen, Manfred von (the 'Red Baron') 27, 30, 60, 80
Robinson, Sgt Robert G. 94
Roe, Alliot Verdon 62
Rolls-Royce **88**, 94
Rolls-Royce Eagle engines 59, 90–1, **90**, 97, 105, 106, 114, 117
Rolls-Royce Falcon engines 79, 81, **82**
Roulers railway station 61
Royal Air Force (RAF) 7, 42, 82–3, 93, **93**, **101**, 111
 and the Airco DH.9A 95, **96**, 100, **100**
 and the Bristol F.2 79
 creation, April 1918 7, 92
 and the Fairey III 119
 and the Felixstowe flying boat 118
 and the Handley Page Type O 107, **107**
 and the Nieuport 27 20
 and the Sopwith Camel 38
 and the Sopwith Snipe 47
 and the SPAD S.XIII 44
 Squadrons
  No. 10 Sqn 78
  No. 39 Sqn **100**
  No. 43 Sqn 47
  No. 45 Sqn **96**
  No. 59 Sqn **74**
  No. 84 Sqn **100**
  No. 99 Sqn 97, **97**, **99**
  No. 100 Sqn 98
  No. 110 Sqn **99**

No. 151 Sqn 37
No. 185 Sqn 101
No. 201 Squadron 47
No. 202 Sqn **91**
No. 207 Sqn **106**
No. 211 Sqn **95**
No. 246 Sqn 102
Royal Aircraft Factory 1A engine 52, 75
Royal Aircraft Factory 1b engine 54
Royal Aircraft Factory 3a engine **90**
Royal Aircraft Factory 4a engine 68, **72**
Royal Aircraft Factory B.E. series 73
Royal Aircraft Factory B.E.1 50
Royal Aircraft Factory B.E.2 49, 50–4, **54**, 68, 72, 76, 79
 Royal Aircraft Factory B.E.2a 50, 57
 Royal Aircraft Factory B.E.2b 50, **50**
 Royal Aircraft Factory B.E.2c 50–2, **51–2**, 54, **54**, 57, **58**, 64, 75, 121, **122**
 Royal Aircraft Factory B.E.2d 53
 Royal Aircraft Factory B.E.2e **52**, 53–4, 73
 Royal Aircraft Factory B.E.2f **53**
Royal Aircraft Factory B.E.9 'pulpit' fighter 54
Royal Aircraft Factory F.E. series 79
Royal Aircraft Factory F.E.2 57–61
 Royal Aircraft Factory F.E.2a 57, 58
 Royal Aircraft Factory F.E.2b 57–9, **57–9**, **58**, 60–1
 Royal Aircraft Factory F.E.2c 59
 Royal Aircraft Factory F.E.2d 59–60, 61, **61**, 79
Royal Aircraft Factory F.E.8 27, **27**
Royal Aircraft Factory R.E.1 68
Royal Aircraft Factory R.E.2 68
Royal Aircraft Factory R.E.3 68
Royal Aircraft Factory R.E.4 68
Royal Aircraft Factory R.E.5 67, **68**
Royal Aircraft Factory R.E.7 67, **68**
Royal Aircraft Factory R.E.8 54, 72–4, **72–4**, 75, 78, 79, 81, 82
Royal Aircraft Factory S.E.5 ('Scout Experimental 5') 20, 26, 39–43, **39**
 Royal Aircraft Factory S.E.5a 9, 26, 27, 34, 39–43, **40**, **41**, **42**, **43**
 Royal Aircraft Factory S.E.5b 42
Royal Aircraft Factory T.E.1 42
Royal Australian Air Force (RAAF) 43
Royal Flying Corps (RFC) 6–7, 13, **14**, 42

and the Airco DH.2 13
and the Airco DH.4 90–2
and the Airco DH.5 26
and the Airco DH.9 95, 96–7
and Avro 63
and the Martinsyde Scout 12
merger with the RNAS to form the RAF 7
and the Morane Saulnier Type L 66
and the Morane Saulnier Type N 15
and the Morane-Saulnier BB 67
and the Nieuport 16 16
and the Nieuport 17 17
and the Nieuport 24 20
and the Nieuport 27 20
and the Royal Aircraft Factory B.E.2c 52–3, **52**
and the Royal Aircraft Factory R.E.8 72
and the Short Bomber **88**
and the Sopwith 1½ Strutter 69, 70, 71
and the Sopwith Camel 33–4
and the Sopwith Pup 23, 24
and the Sopwith Tabloid 10
and the SPAD S.VII 31, 32
and the SPAD S.XIII 44
Squadrons
 No. 2 Sqn 50, 78
 No. 4 Sqn 52–3
 No. 5 Sqn **56**, 63
 No. 6 Sqn 58
 No. 8 Sqn 52
 No. 10 Sqn **53**
 No. 11 Sqn 55, **57**
 No. 12 Sqn **51**
 No. 16 Sqn **73**
 No. 18 Sqn **90**
 No. 19 Sqn 45, 54
 No. 20 Sqn 58, 83
 No. 21 Sqn **74**
 No. 22 Sqn **58**
 No. 23 Sqn 44
 No. 24 Sqn 26, 42
 No. 25 Sqn 59
 No. 27 Sqn 89
 No. 33 Sqn **64**
 No. 35 Sqn **76**, 78
 No. 40 Sqn 27
 No. 41 Sqn 27
 No. 45 Sqn **70**
 No. 47 Sqn 75
 No. 48 Sqn 79–80
 No. 52 Sqn 73
 No. 54 Sqn 23
 No. 55 Sqn 91
 No. 56 Sqn 39, 40
 No. 57 Sqn **61**
 No. 59 Sqn 73
 No. 65 Sqn **62**
 No. 66 Sqn **35**

No. 70 Sqn 33, 70
No. 100 Sqn **58**
No. 102 Sqn 61
No. 104 Sqn (later No. 104 Sqn RAF) **96**, 97
No. 111 Sqn **79**
No. 139 Sqn **80**, **83**
and the Vickers F.B.5 'Gunbus' 55
and the Vickers FB.19 22
and the Voisin LA 87
Royal Naval Air Service (RNAS) 6–7, 18
and the Airco DH.4 90–2, **91–4**
and airships 122, 123
and the Caudron G.4 104, **104**
and the Curtiss flying boat 116, 117
and the Fairey Campania 114
and the Farman MF.11 86
Flights, 'B' Flight 10 Naval Sqn (the 'Black Flight') 30
and the Handley Page Type O 105–6, **105**, **107**
merger with the RFC to form the RAF 7
and the Morane Saulnier Type L 66
and the Morane-Saulnier BB 67, **67**
and the Nieuport 10 and 11 16
and the Nieuport 17 17
and the Norman Thompson N.T.4 115
and the Royal Aircraft Factory B.E.2c **51**
and the Short Bomber 88
and the Sopwith 1½ Strutter 69, 70, 71, **71**, 119
and the Sopwith Camel 33, 34–6
and the Sopwith and Fairey Hamble Baby 113
and the Sopwith Pup 23, 24
and the Sopwith Schneider 10
and the Sopwith T.1 Cuckoo 101
and the Sopwith Tabloid 10
and the Sopwith Triplane 24, 29
Squadrons
 No. 1 Naval Sqn 30
 No. 2 Sqn 30
 No. 4 Sqn 33, **67**
 No. 5 Sqn **91**, **93**
 No. 6 Sqn 97
 No. 7 Naval Sqn 104
 No. 7 Sqn 88, **105**, 106
 No. 7A Sqn 106
 No. 8 Sqn 23
Wings
 No. 2 Wing **94**
 No. 3 Wing **71**
 No. 5 Wing 70, 106
Royal Naval Flying School, Vendrome aerodrome **65**

126

INDEX

Royal Navy 11, 23–4, 35, 85, 88, 109, 112, 114, 116–17, 119–21
Royal Navy Air Department 101, 105
Russia 17, 22, 24, 30, 65, 67, 86, 87, 91, 104
Russian Civil War 22, 38, 100, 114, 119
Ruston Proctor, Lincoln **54**, 70
Rutland, Flt Cdr F. J. **9**

SABCA 83
SACA 46
Salmson 2 71
Salonika 75
Savage, John 'Mad Jack' 43
Savage Wolseley S.E.5a 43
Scapa Flow 114, **123**
Scarff, F. W. **98**
Scarff ring **98**
Schlichting, Sgt Wilhelm 87
Schneider Trophy 10, 119
Schütte-Lanz SL 11 54
Science Museum, London 43
S.E. Saunders 116, 117
seaplanes 109–20
Second World War 7
'sesquiplane' 16, 20
Short, Horace 110
Short 166 88
Short Bomber 88, **88**
Short Brothers 88
Short 'Folder' seaplanes 110–11, **110–11**
    Short Admiralty Type 166 110
    Short S.41 110
    Short S.81 110
    Short Type 184 88, 110–11, **110**
    Short Type 320 111
    Short Type 827 110, **111**
Siemens-Schuckert D.I. 17
Sigrist, Fred 69
single-seat fighters 9–47, 54, 56
skywriting 43
Smith, Herbert 29, 33, 45, 69
Smith, Keith 103
Smith, Ross 103
Somme campaign 15, 70, 88, 89
Sopwith 1½ Strutter (Type 9700) **49**, 69–71, **69–71**, 79, 104, 119
    SOP. 1A.2 71
    SOP. 1B.1 71
    SOP. 1B.2 71
Sopwith 5F.1 Dolphin 45–6, **45**, **46**
Sopwith Aviation Company 7
Sopwith 'Big Pup' *see* Sopwith Camel
Sopwith Dolphin 44
    Mk.I 46
    Mk.II 46
    Mk.III 46
Sopwith Dove 24

Sopwith F.1 Camel **6**, 7, 9, 24, 26, 28, 30, 33–9, **33–6**, **38**, 47, 70
Sopwith 2F.1 'Ship's Camel' 35–6, **36**, 120
Sopwith Camel 'Comic' 36–7, 70
Sopwith and Fairey Hamble Baby 112–13, **112–13**
Sopwith and Fairey Hamble Baby Convert 113
Sopwith LCT 69
Sopwith Pup 7, **9**, 23–4, **23**–5, 26, 29, 33, 120
Sopwith Schneider 10, 112
Sopwith Scout 23
    see also Sopwith Pup
Sopwith Snipe 37, 38, 47, **47**
Sopwith T.1 Cuckoo 101, **101**
Sopwith Tabloid 10, **10**, 12, 69
Sopwith T.F.1 ('Trench Fighter 1') 38
Sopwith T.F.2 Salamander 7, 38, 47
Sopwith 'Training Camel' 34
Sopwith Triplane ('Tripe-hound'/'Tripe') 18, 24, 29–30, **29**, **30**
Soviet Union 38, 64, 91, 100, 119
SPAD 21
SPAD S.VII 20, 22, 31–2, **31–2**, 44
SPAD S.XII 42
SPAD S.XIII 34, 44, 46
Spurling, Lt. Arthur 97
SS Class ('Submarine Scout') airship 121–2, **122**, 123
SSP class (airship) 122
SST class (airship) 122
SSZ (Sea Scout Zero) 65 **121**, 122
Stagg, Air Mechanic A. T. C. **80**
Standard Aircraft Corporation 94
Standard Motor Company 23
Strange, Captain Louis 12
Strasser, Peter 92
strategic bomber force, land-based 7
Stubbs, Capt John Stevenson 97
Sueter, Capt Murray 105
Sueter, Cdre Murray 101
Suk, Grigory 22
Sunbeam 78, **88**
Sunbeam Arab engines 74, 81–2
Sunbeam Cossack engines 118
Sunbeam Maori engines 114
Sunbeam Nubian engines 110
Supermarine aircraft company 53

Talbot, 2nd Lt Ralph 94
Taube monoplane 63
Tennant, Capt 53
Tønder 36
Torpedo Aeroplane School **101**
Travers, Captain Frederick Dudley 28
Trenchard 80
Trenchard, Hugh 95

Trier railway station **58**
Turkish forces 12, 111
two-seater fighters & reconnaissance 49–82

U-boats 6, 102, **102**, 109, 117, 121–3
    UB-12 93
    UB-115 123
    UC-70 102
United States 38, 42–3, 44, 83, 92, 93–4, 98, 117, 118
    25th Aero Squadron 42
United States Army Air Corps (USAAC) 43, 94
United States Army Air Service (USAAS) 93–4
United States Marine Corps 94
    Northern Bombing Group 98–100
United States Navy 43, 94, 117, 118
United States Post Office 94
Upavon 23
Uruguay 21

Versailles treaty talks 93
Vickers 50, 70
Vickers 'Destroyer' (E.F.B.1) 55
Vickers D.H.2 6, 9
Vickers E.S.1 (Experimental Scout 1) 22
Vickers F.B.5 'Gunbus' 6, 55–6, **55–6**, 59
Vickers F.B.9 56
Vickers F.B.19 (the Bullet/'Vickers Bullitt') 22, **22**
Vickers F.E.2b 56
Vickers guns 16, 17, 20, 23, 33, 35, 36, 41, 43, 45, **56**, 60, 69, 72, 78, 81
Vickers Instructional Machine 61
Vickers Vimy 103, 107
    Vickers Vimy I **103**
Victoria Cross 11, 18, 47, 66, **66**, **68**, 78
Villers-Bretonneux 55
Vincent, Jesse G. **99**
Vindex (early aircraft carrier) 11, 70
Voisin III 87, **87**
Voisin L 87
Voisin LA 87, **87**
Voisin LAS 87
Voisin pusher aircraft 50

War Office 11, 28, 63
Waring, Lt **102**
Warneford, Sub Lt Reginald **66**
Warsaw, battle of 83
Waziristan 100
Wellington bomber 103
Western Front 12, **14**, 16, 21–3, 28, 32, 34–5, 51, 65, 75, 78–9, 86–7
Westgate-on-Sea 119

Westland Aircraft company 95, 98, **98–9**
Westland Walrus 100
Westland Wapiti 100
White Finnish 114
White Russian forces 38
Whitehead 23
Whitten-Brown, Arthur 103
Wiesbaden 106
Willows, Ernest 121
Willows airships 121
Wilson, 2nd Lt C. W. 63
Wolseley engines 50
Wolseley Viper 40
Woodbridge, 2nd Lt A. E. 60
Wright 43

Yarmouth (modified frigate) **9**, 24

Zangen, Oberleutnant Fritz von 87
Zeebrugge Mole 88
Zeppelin works, Friedrichshafen 63–4
Zeppelins 6, 11, 54, 61, 70, 90, 92, 113, 117
    factory air raids on 10, 63–4
    Zeppelin L 23 24
    Zeppelin L 33 123
    Zeppelin L 54 36
    Zeppelin L 60 36
    Zeppelin L 70 92
    Zeppelin LZ 25 10
    Zeppelin LZ 37 66, **66**

Picture credits

AirSeaLand Images: 6, 8, 12, 24, 29, 35, 85, 86
Alamy: 7, 46, 48, 54, 89, 101, 108, 111, 112
Getty Images: 122, 123
Naval History & Heritage Command: 71
Public Domain: 14, 31, 100, 104

ARTWORK CREDITS:

Amber Books Ltd: 13, 21 (both), 25 (top), 32 (both), 38 (both), 43 (both), 54, 59, 72–73, 75, 81, 96 (lower), 102–103, 107 (top & middle), 120–123

Edward Ward: 115

Ronny Bar: 5, 10–11, 14–20, 22–23, 24–25 (lower), 26–31, 33–37, 39–42, 44–53, 55–58, 60–71, 74 (both), 76–80, 82–95, 96 (top), 97–99, 105, 106–107 (lower), 110–114, 116–119